BRAIN SELL

The authors wish to acknowledge
all the great sales brains around the globe
for their brilliant ideas and suggestions
that have made *Brain Sell* possible.

BRAIN SELL

Tony Buzan and Richard Israel

Gower

Published by
Gower Publishing Limited
Gower House
Croft Road
Aldershot
Hampshire GU11 3HR
England

Gower
Old Post Road
Brookfield
Vermont 05036
USA

Reprinted 2000

Tony Buzan and Richard Israel have asserted their right under the Copyright, Designs and Patents Act 1988 to be identified as the author of this work.

Vanda North – Mind Map Artist
Malcolm Stern – Editorial Director
Solveig Gardner Servian – Managing Editor
Linda Cayford – Copy-Editor
Dorothy Stewart – Proofreader
Michael Heary – Indexer
FdK Design Consultants – Jacket Design

British Library Cataloguing in Publication Data
Buzan, Tony
 Brain Sell
 I. Title II. Israel, Richard
 658.8

ISBN 0–566–07658–6 Hardback
    0–566–07667–5 Paperback

Library of Congress Cataloging-in-Publication Data
Buzan, Tony.
 Brain sell / Tony Buzan and Richard Israel.
    p.   cm.
 ISBN 0–566–07858–6. — ISBN 0–566–07667–5 (pbk.)
 1. Selling. I. Israel, Richard. II. Title.
HF5438.25.B89   1995
 658.85—dc20
                                                                            94–47402
                                                                            CIP

Typeset in Palatino by Poole Typesetting (Wessex) Ltd, Bournemouth and printed by Bookcraft (Bath) Ltd, Midsomer Norton, Somerset

The Authors

Tony Buzan enjoys an international reputation as the leading writer, teacher and lecturer on enhancing the effectiveness of the mind. His books have been published in more than fifty countries and translated into twenty languages. One of them – *Use Your Head* – has sold over a million copies. He is the originator of Mind Maps® and makes frequent television appearances around the world. He is also much in demand as an adviser to corporate and government leaders worldwide.

Richard Israel is an acknowledged authority on instructional design, and pioneer of the use of behaviour modelling to improve selling skills. More than one and a half million people, on four continents, have been trained with his materials. He has written three books and numerous articles and lectures widely on sales training.

Contents

List of figures

Skill Builders

Preface

All sales are simply a brain-to-brain exchange – the salesperson's brain communicating with the customer's. It is only in recent years that much new information has become available on the latest research in the fields of psychology, communications, general science, sports and Olympic training techniques, neurophysiology, brain research, sales research and selling techniques.

Our purpose is to bring you this new information, as it relates to sales and communication, in a novel and original way. Our objective is to make this information easy to understand and easy to master. Once you comprehend it and incorporate it into your everyday sales behaviours, you'll enjoy getting more of whatever you want. To this end we have included a series of 94 exercises, called 'skill builders'. Each one is designed to follow and expand on the previous one, resulting in a complete *Brain Sell* self-development programme.

Brain Sell is divided into four distinct Parts. Each Part is self-contained and designed for you to master before proceeding to the next. If you have no previous sales experience we take you through the basics of selling in the Appendix to Part One. If you are a seasoned sales professional, you'll discover new information from the very first chapter. A series of quizzes enables you to assess your current knowledge and performance levels. *Brain Sell* presents, for the first time, an in-depth approach to the 'art' and 'science' of selling. You will also discover how to become an information expert in the ever-expanding global knowledge economy.

Among *Brain Sell*'s unique features is a new communication and sales concept incorporated in a revolutionary manner. You learn secrets from the master salespeople with whom we have worked over the years. You travel from the medical laboratories of brain research, to *the last four feet* – the distance between you and your customer – as you apply this breakthrough research to your selling activities.

The new sales tools – the Sales Mind Matrix, the truth-seeking brain, Infoswap, Mind Maps®, sales memory and the Sales Compass – are all designed to increase your brain and sales power. You enter the training camps of Olympic athletes, and learn how to apply their visualization techniques to your personal development. You become a sales detective, infallibly solving the case (satisfying the customer).

We trust you will enjoy the exciting journey that the following pages provide. As you explore, develop and profit from the better use of your truly magnificent creative brain cells, you will become a 'SuperSellf'.

Tony Buzan and Richard Israel

Authors' notes

Chapter summaries appearing at the end of each chapter, after the Reviews, are in the form of Mind Maps®. Mind Maps are explained in depth in Part Two: Information: The New Wealth. The main points of the chapter are understood if one starts with a general concept in the centre of the page and branches out using words, images, colours and symbols to represent the more detailed points which are related and connected to each other. The Mind Maps will serve as an excellent review of each chapter and have been shown to improve the ability to memorize the material significantly.

In this book, the pronouns 'he' and 'she' are used interchangeably. Examples are given throughout using both genders equally. Nothing should be inferred about the relationship between particular characteristics and either sex.

The authors wish to acknowledge all the great sales brains around the globe for their brilliant ideas and suggestions that have made *Brain Sell* possible.

TB
RI

PART ONE

The Sales Mind Matrix and sales memory

Introduction

Brain Sell will help you to sell, using your whole creative brain. You may have experienced a nagging thought in the back of your mind that your sales career should be a glowing success and that life has more to offer ... if only you knew how! The good news is that 'the how' has now arrived. The following pages offer you effective new formulas designed to help develop the untapped potential of your brain. Your sales will achieve undreamed of heights.

Your brain is like a sleeping giant. In recent years, researchers in psychology, education, sports and mathematics have shown that its potential is far greater than imagined. Even the commonly heard statement that, on average, we use only 1 per cent of our brains, may be an overestimate, as it now appears that we use even less than 1 per cent – which means that an enormous amount of your capability is still available for development. (For more details see Tony Buzan's *The Mind Map Book*, BBC Publications.)

When you began your sales career, were you thrown in at the deep end, with no formal instruction, in a 'sink or swim' situation? Were you allocated a senior salesperson to study and follow around? Did you undertake some type of formal sales training programme or were you merely given a sales book to read? Did you go to sales meetings and become enthused, only to fall flat again?

Of the people taking up the six million new sales positions expected to be created worldwide in the 1990s, only 10 per cent will receive any formal instruction, and much of that instruction will be outdated! The result?

Many salespeople will be unhappy with their present sales positions and will spend a good deal of each day considering a change of career!

Skill Builder 1: self-check

The following Yes/No questions give you some awareness of your present state of mind regarding selling. Record your answers as you go along.

	YES	NO
1. Do you enjoy your work?		
2. Are you excited about going to work each morning?		
3. Are you full of energy all day?		
4. Can you stay focused on each customer you sell to?		
5. Do you remember all your customers' names and faces?		
6. Do you remember the important details about your regular customers' businesses and personal lives, including birthdays, anniversaries, children's names and pets' names?		
7. Do you remember what your last eight customers bought from you?		
8. Do you have creative, original and personal methods for planning your sales presentation?		
9. Do you have creative, original and personal methods for giving your sales presentation?		
10. Have you made a concentrated study of your brain and how it works?		
11. Are you in the top 5 per cent of salespeople in your company?		
12. Can you remember what each customer says to you?		
13. Do your returning customers ask for you by name?		
14. Do you believe you are worth more than you earn?		
15. Do you feel good about yourself and the use of your potential?		
16. Are you able to turn your daydreams into reality?		
17. Are your sales presentations memorable?		
18. Do you understand the nature of communication and how it affects your sales results?		

	YES	NO
19. Are you one of the top experts in knowledge about your own and your competition's products, and services?		
20. Are you physically and mentally fit?		
TOTAL SCORE		

If you scored more than 17 'yeses' you are in good shape and *Brain Sell* can help move you to the top. If you are below 17 'yeses', work that extra bit harder and *Brain Sell* will revolutionize the way you sell bringing you financial and job satisfaction.

As mentioned before, *Brain Sell* is in four Parts. Each Part contains those distinct skills and knowledge necessary in *the last four feet* – the distance between the customer and the salesperson, the space in which sales are made or lost. Once you have mastered the skills in *Brain Sell* you will be able to apply them to any aspect of selling: a telephone sales conversation, a home shopping network on television, a sales letter or face-to-face selling.

Part One provides an in-depth understanding of the miraculous brain. After studying a few chapters and putting these simple and powerful *Brain Sell* sales techniques to work, you will be selling in new and exciting ways.

Chapter 1 is called 'Whole-brain Selling: Sales Mind Matrix to increase sales'. The Sales Mind Matrix covers ten different mental skills of your whole creative brain. The customer's brain is 'truth-seeking' and needs the correct information to make the right decisions. You, the salesperson, must be able to supply this information to ensure you make the most of the unlimited sales opportunities that lie ahead.

Chapter 2 has the title 'Salesenses. Make your Senses Sell'. Sales are made and lost in *the last four feet*. You will learn how information enters your brain through your senses and how it can be communicated back to your customers' five senses for maximum sales effect.

Chapter 3 is 'Memory Imprints. "I Remember YOU!"'. What impression do your customers make on your brain? How is this impression influenced? How can you make that impression last forever? This section explains how to remember customers' names and faces. With two simple techniques you will make a lasting mental impression on all your customers.

In introducing your whole creative brain to the sales process, you will unleash a new force in your life. Whole-brain selling leads to whole-brain creative thinking, and your perspective and behaviour will change in many pleasant ways. You will shift away from the old supply-and-demand model to one of limitless opportunity and abundance. You will think creatively about new opportunities and will take the corresponding action. There are five and a half billion customers out there. Each one of those customers buys products and services daily. Are you part of this cycle? Are you building your sales career, your wealth and your future by tapping into this dynamic economic process of buying and selling? Are you using *Brain Sell* sales skills?

Part One will show you how to become a high producer – a knowledge-able salesperson who ensures that customers get what they want, resulting in increased sales performance. *Brain Sell* will also teach you how your customers' minds work, based on the latest scientific research on the brain and the experiences of some of the world's top sales producers.

Brain Sell is for everyone, regardless of experience or the type of products, services or ideas sold. When you have mastered *Brain Sell*, you will be well on your way to achieving higher sales. You'll enjoy your work with less stress, while building a base of loyal customers who will keep returning to you.

The chapters in Part One will show how you can:

● communicate better;
● turn ordinary information into a living experience;
● change your brain power into selling power;
● remember your customers' names and personal details;
● use the keys to memory;
● enjoy effective, fun-filled workdays;
● remember your customers' needs;
● have unlimited *satisfied* customers.

Each of the three chapters contains Skill Builders, all designed to help you sell better. To make the best use of the material, first, skim through it rapidly to get a general understanding. Then read it in depth and do all the Skill Builders in the proper sequence. For maximum benefit we recommend that you spend a week on each chapter, giving yourself time for in-depth reading, study, practice-time for the Skill Builders and time for your brain to absorb and integrate all the new material into your everyday sales behaviours.

To speed up the mastery of these new materials we strongly recommend that you talk about them to your family, friends and peers at work. If you belong to a club, association or group, make a short presentation on any aspect of the book you wish. This will allow you to practise many skills in the book, and the results will delight you.

When you have finished the in-depth reading, keep the book with you for daily reference. You will be surprised at the new thoughts, new ideas and new techniques you will develop. Keep a record of these new thoughts and ideas. Complete the Sales Management section found in Appendix A at the back of the book (page 243). And finally, please write to us with your successes, stories and ideas, at the address given in Appendix B.

As you work your way through *Brain Sell* you will learn many new skills. Tony and Richard have trained salespeople over a combined total of 55 years, and have learned that it's important to practise new skills for mastery.

Let's stop for a moment and complete a simple experiment. First, fold your arms. Now, fold your arms the other away around. That is, if you had them folded left over right, reverse it to right over left or vice versa. When you folded your arms the second time, did it feel a little awkward?

When you learn any new skill, there may be a similar 'awkward period'. It is natural to want to return to the old ways that seem comfortable. Mastering the new skills in *Brain Sell* takes persistence and practice.

Persistence requires taking *Brain Sell* seriously, and practice. Practise what? We have given you over 21 skill-building exercises. The serious student of *Brain Sell* will do each one. Take your time: this is an investment in your career and future. Practising these newly acquired skills in your daily life will take conscious effort until they become part of your everyday behavioural repertoire.

If you are new to selling or want to review fundamentals, we have included 'Sales Basics' in the Appendix on page 65. Before you cover 'Sales Basics', complete Chapters 1 and 2. One way to speed up this process is to review continually the materials and Skill Builders. We recommend that you review each chapter as soon as you complete it, as advised in the chapter summaries. This technique will help you to move *Brain Sell* into your long-term memory. At the end of each chapter we give a summary in the form of a Mind Map.

Regard *Brain Sell* as an exciting journey, an adventure of discovery into that *last four feet*. The pay-off will be enjoying that new car, that exotic vacation, that special relationship or whatever else you want from life.

Finally, to complete this Introduction, here is your Skill Builder review.

Skill Builder 2: introduction review

On a separate piece of blank paper, summarize the Introduction. You may look back.

1 Whole-brain selling

Sales Mind Matrix to increase sales

A certain smile

Imagine you are in Paris and decide to visit the Louvre. Once inside you find wonderful works of art and fascinating groups of people gathered from all corners of the world. You follow one group, listening to their guide, as he gives intriguing accounts of both the art and the artist.

'And here we have the *Mona Lisa*, painted by the amazing Leonardo da Vinci', explains the guide. You look up in awe at a grand, priceless work of art.

'Leonardo was born in 1452 near Florence, Italy where he spent the first thirty years of his life ...' Your mind drifts back to this extraordinary time in history, the Florentine Renaissance. 'Leonardo was a master at art, sculpture, physiology, general science, architecture, mechanics, anatomy, physics, invention, meteorology, geology, engineering and aviation. He could spontaneously compose, play and sing songs.'

As the group listens in rapt attention, a strange feeling overcomes you ...

'Leonardo had a perfect, balanced, well developed body, including a brilliant brain that allowed him to do so much ...'

As the guide speaks, you feel a little dizzy and as you close your eyes you hear, loud and clear in your head, an unfamiliar strong, wonderfully inspiring voice, which says, 'Yes my friend, you have a brilliant brain, a brain which can do all the things I have.' Quickly opening your eyes, you glance up at the *Mona Lisa*, only to observe her lips move, ever so slightly, giving you that famous smile. A cold shiver runs down your spine, for on that day, in Paris, you have heard the voice of a Master. You have heard The Truth.

Overview

This first chapter includes self-checks to help you find out whether or not you are currently using all your brain power in your sales. You will study the Sales Mind Matrix and the ten mental skills that you can apply with every future customer contact, resulting in accurate information gathering and clearer communication. Understand that the customer's brain is 'truth seeking', needing the correct data to make the right decisions. You, the salesperson, need to provide this information to ensure that you make the most of the unlimited sales opportunities that lie ahead.

Miracles of your brain

The phenomenal organ we call the brain weighs less than three pounds – that is, about the same weight as a laptop computer. And that's where any comparison with a computer ends. Your brain has the capacity to store more information than all the libraries in the world. Your brain can make your feet dance to Elton John, your lips hum to John Denver, and tears fill your eyes to Barbra Streisand. As you look around at the incredible man-made items in your life – cars, planes, televisions, computers, skyscrapers, satellites, books, art, sculpture – remember, they all originated from brains!

Your brain can do anything you can imagine, once you know how to use it. How well have you been using it up to now?

Skill Builder 3: check your sales ability

Read each question, and tick (✔) the appropriate 'yes' or 'no' answer. Be honest with yourself to get accurate feedback.

	YES	NO
1. Do you have a clear vision of how your company, customers, and yourself expect you to sell?		
2. Do you find yourself tapping out a rhythm or humming a tune during your work?		

	YES	NO

3. Do you want to be of service to your customers?
4. Do you have daydreams of the perfect customer and the perfect sale?
5. Do you have great ideas of how to increase sales?
6. Have you noticed that sometimes a customer will buy from you because he likes you?
7. Have you felt that you could increase your sales if you were able to change some company's rules?
8. Do you have certain customers who think like you, buy from you and are a pleasure to deal with?
9. Do you plan each day and set goals?
10. Do you learn something from every customer contact?
11. Have you experienced thinking you knew what the customer wanted and found you were right?
12. Do you remember all your customers' names and faces?
13. Do you have customers whom you can call on the phone and chat with, without fear of being rejected?
14. Do you feel that your full potential is used in your present position?
15. Do you tell the truth in your sales conversations?
16. Do you have in-depth knowledge about the products and services you sell?
17. Do you believe the public has a high regard for successful salespeople?
18. Do you find new and interesting ways to present your sales story every day?
19. Do you believe in the goods and services you are selling?
20. During the day, do you dream about new ways of building your customer base and your career?

TOTAL SCORE

If, you scored more than 17 'yeses' you are well on your way to becoming a Master Salesperson. If you scored below 17 *Brain Sell* will be of enormous value to you.

Your whole brain

Consider for a moment what a customer's and a salesperson's brains do in the sales process. They accept information, sort and store it, then they add to it and exchange it again. So, understanding how we receive, store and send information including the information itself, is an important subject for sales success.

The listener – your customer – receives this information using all her senses. However, she now processes and stores that information in a more complex manner. To understand this, you should become more familiar with the brain and how it works.

The outer part of your brain (cerebral cortex) is divided into two halves, the left and the right. Recent researches by Dr Robert Ornstein of the University of California, based on the Nobel-prize-winning work of Dr Roger Sperry at the California Institute of Technology, have thrown more light on the different activities handled by each side of the brain. We now know that the brain has many different mental skills for the processing and storing of information:

Right cortex	**Left cortex**
pictures	numbers
imagination	words
colour	logic
rhythm	lists
space	details

Figure 1.1   The brain's cerebral cortex shown face-on

Let's consider how each of these mental skills can apply to our everyday sales:

- *Numbers* are used for prices and discounts and keeping records.
- *Words* are used in sales conversations: irrespective of what language you are speaking you use words. In advertising you use words to convey your sales message.
- *Logic* should always be present in your sale. The first logical step in the sales presentation is the greeting or gaining the customer's attention.
- *Lists* are used for prices and sizes and references. Lists help keep track and give order to the masses of information you handle.
- *Details* are important to ensure customers receive exactly what they want. Details can be sizes, colours, specifications, and sometimes details appear endless!
- *Pictures* are used in sales catalogues and advertisements. Good salespeople are able to paint pictures in their customers' minds!
- *Imagination* is used constantly in sales advertisements, where the customer imagines owning a new home, driving a new car or enjoying peace of mind.
- *Colour* in sales can be in packaging, catalogues, advertisements and, of course, colourful sales presentations!
- *Rhythm* can refer to the rhythm of the sale conversation where the salesperson and the customers appear to be in synchronization. The rhythm of your voice makes it both interesting to listen to and memorable.
- *Space* has many different meanings. In advertising this could be the layout – one that is not too cramped and is easy to read. In face-to-face selling it could be the distance between the customer and the salesperson, the last four feet.

A full explanation of how each of the above mental skills applies to selling starts on page 15.

The sales Mind Matrix-1

Recent research shows that the brain acts as a WHOLE, *with all the mental skills supporting each other*. We represent this with the Sales Mind Matrix (see Figure 1.2).

	0%	25%	50%	75%	100%	
Numbers						TOTALS
Words						
Logic						
Lists						
Details						
Pictures						TOTALS
Imagination						
Colour						
Rhythm						
Space						

Figure 1.2   Sales Mind Matrix

Skill Builder 4: your Sales Mind Matrix

Complete the above Sales Mind Matrix by considering each of your ten mental skills, one at a time. For example ask yourself, 'How aware am I of the use of *numbers* when I'm selling?' If you think about 50 per cent, shade in the area (up to 50 per cent), and write in 50. Move on to the next mental skill, *words*, repeating the previous question but substitute 'words' for 'numbers'. Shade in your score and write the number. Continue until you have considered all ten mental skills.

Now add the total score for the first five mental skills, from *numbers* to *details*. Write the total score in the right hand shaded column.

Next add up your total score for the remaining mental skills, from *pictures* to *space*. Write the total score in the right-hand shaded column.

How did you do? If you have shaded equally both the top set (the left cortical mental skills) and the bottom set (the right cortical mental skills), you are using a whole creative brain approach. But if one set has a higher score and is more shaded than the other you can immediately see your own areas to improve! Obviously using all your mental skills at 100 per cent will result in superior sales performance.

Next consider how the Sales Mind Matrix applies to your customer. Just as you have your own profile, so each of your customers will have his or her unique profile. We will explain these implications in the Brain Sell Compass (Part Three, Chapter 9).

Let's examine the Sales Mind Matrix by first understanding how each mental skill works in a sale, then how to make all the mental skills work for you.

Numbers

Numbers play an important role in your life. Your pay cheque and bank balance are all in numbers! Prices, profits, discounts, sizes, measurements, market position, market share, phone numbers, addresses, ages, catalogues, references, code numbers, the stock market, the price of gold, today's temperature, and in sports the scores are in numbers. Numbers give us feedback and comparisons. We measure time, days, weeks, months, years in numbers.

Words

Words play a vital role in our lives. Not only do we communicate with words but we think with words and use words in our 'self-talk'. Words can make us laugh and cry, can move us to action or inaction, give us hope or despair. Words are the tools of our trade, making up the languages we speak to our customers. Think of your favourite salesperson and the words she or he uses with you!

We use words to express our ideas, our concerns and our dreams. Words are one of the main building blocks of our communication skills. The right words can make or break a sales presentation!

Logic

Logic reflects the brain's ability to reason. In selling you use logic as a detective would use detecting skills. For example, if you receive repeated requests for a specific product or service you do not offer, the logical approach is to find and make a similar product or service available to your customers.

A logical approach to a sales presentation is to make an appointment, know the correct address and have the directions to get there. Ensure that you have all the necessary sales materials with you – price lists, samples, brochures – before you leave the office. Here you are using reason or logic to plan the sales presentation in the most effective way.

Lists

Do you enjoy reading the 'top 20' hit tunes each week? Or the 'top ten' best selling books? Or the 'top ten' best performing stocks? If so, you are actually enjoying lists! Lists give order and priority. Lists can take the forms of tables, for example of planes, train and bus times. Lists can be ranges, from shoe size to wine vintages and prices. Lists can be cross references – what type of film to use with different camera settings. Lists give you an instant grasp of a number of items.

Lists enable you to give specific information to your customer in a concise and efficient manner, for example price lists, stock lists, delivery schedules.

Details

The human brain loves the details that complete the total picture. With details missing something just doesn't feel right. Getting all the details can be laborious, yet it makes the world of difference. The Japanese provide a good example of this. If you study products made in Japan you will notice how good they are on details. Making certain that every little detail is just right is one of the principal reasons for the successful sales of their cars around the world.

Think of your favourite restaurant. Does it have fresh flowers on the table, shiny silverware, staff in clean uniforms? You can see how important the details are to an overall quality experience in the service and product industries. Details are not just minor considerations. Together they *are* the product.

Pictures

'One picture is worth a thousand words' is an expression you have often heard. Pictures can convey so much information in an instant. Our earliest record of communication – cave drawings – are in pictures. It is the pictures in magazine and newspaper advertisements that form messages, moods and feelings which all create the desire to buy. Pictures are the means by which we store information in our long-term memory. Can you close your eyes and picture the front door of your home?

The skilful salesperson paints word-pictures in his or her customer's mind, in the same way as looking in a mirror gives you a clear picture of how a new item of clothing looks on you.

Imagination

How often have you bought a product or service simply because you imagined how great it would be to own or enjoy it? That exercise programme as you imagined your body becoming fit and trim! That new dream kitchen in a magazine, full of all the latest appliances! That once-in-a-lifetime dream vacation to the Bahamas aboard the Love Boat! Yes, imagination is a powerful sales tool that can be very attractive to your customer.

Colour

Colour plays an important part in our lives. It makes our lives exciting, interesting and, yes, colourful! Can you imagine a world made up of only black and white? Look around your sales area to see the effective use of colour. How colourful is your office? Your promotional materials? The packaging of your products? On your next visit to the supermarket notice how important colour is to packaging and marketing of food.

How about *your* packaging: your clothes and your personality? Are they as colourful as they can be? Colour has many roles in sales, including in the speech we use. Colourful speech excites and interests your customer.

Rhythm

Rhythm is integral to our lives. We live our lives in the rhythm of time – hours, days, weeks, months and seasons. Sleeping, working and eating are all part of this natural rhythm. We all love to express rhythm through our bodies by dancing. We speak about being in rhythm or out of rhythm with our customers. The natural rhythm of selling is knowing when to ask questions, when to stay silent, when to demonstrate and when to ask for an order.

What about the rhythm of your sales voice? Do you prefer to listen to someone selling to you in a boring, dull, monotone, colourless voice or one like a musical instrument, rich in tones and textures, moving up and down the scale, keeping you interested and hanging on for the next word? Great speakers, such as Kennedy, Churchill and Luther King, used the rhythm of voice to captivate their audience.

Space

The perception of space is used to judge the distance between objects. When you dance, walk or run you are using this skill. This thinking function enables you to know where to place your hand to lift your cup of coffee without spilling it. The perception of space makes you conscious of your surroundings, your products, customers, yourself and your movements and the movements of others.

Watch how a customer uses his space, how he moves to see items, moving back to see the whole item and forward to see its details, how he or she moves towards you for attention and away from you to create distance. You are observing a dance – yes, a dance. If you videotaped each customer, replayed the tape at different speeds and added appropriate music you would see a unique dance develop for each one. Once you are space-aware you can learn their steps and dance in harmony with each customer!

Skill Builder 5: sales applications

List below ways you can improve your sales using each of the ten mental skills:

1. *Numbers*

2. *Words*

3. *Logic*

4. *Lists*

5. *Details*

6. *Pictures*

7. *Imagination*

8. *Colour*

9. *Rhythm*

10. *Space*

The Sales Mind Matrix in advertising

The Sales Mind Matrix is a foundation skill of *Brain Sell*. Understanding and implementing it in your everyday sales work is critical to your success. We shall be referring to it throughout this book, so start becoming aware of how the Sales Mind Matrix is used in different sales situations.

Dream your dreams

In the recession-hit property market of 1991, Schweppe & Co. of New Jersey sold more houses – 550 – than it did in 1986, its best year for property sales in that decade. Owner, 44-year-old Jay Schweppe, must be doing something right to enjoy these results. Take his advertisement for example. Jay explained to *The Wall Street Journal*, 'I'm not going to put an ad in the paper that says "3,500 square foot home, 2 baths ..." he says. I'll say, "Cozy Tudor nestled in the hillside overlooking the New York skyline. Leaded glass windows and inglenook fireplace. Come dream your dreams here."' Jay Schweppe has many interested buyers phoning his office to find out more. Which of his readers' mental skills is he appealing to? Why, *imagination* as well as *pictures, space, words, logic* and *numbers*. His competitors continue to advertise the '3,500 square foot home, 2 baths', appealing only to *logic, numbers* and *words*.

You must constantly ask yourself:

● Which of my Sales Mind Matrix skills am I currently using?
● How can I incorporate more of my Sales Mind Matrix skills into my selling?

The Sales Mind Matrix can be used in many ways, and advertising is a good example. When you see an advertisement that appeals to you, consider which Sales Mind Matrix skills are being used. When examining the advertisement you could ask a series of questions:

● Have numbers been effectively used?
● Have words been effectively used?
● Has logic been effectively used?

And so on, until you have covered all ten mental skills.

Skill Builder 6: check that ad

Select a magazine or newspaper and browse through. Look for two advertisements: one that you really like and one that you don't. When you have made your selection analyse the first one, the one you really like, against the Sales Mind Matrix (see Figure 1.3). Ask yourself if *numbers* have been used and then shade in the appropriate score: if you think it's 50 per cent, then shade in up to 50 per cent. Next do the same for *words* and then *logic*, next *lists*, until you have covered all ten mental skills. Study the advertisement carefully before you start, and write in the title of the advertisement for future reference.

REALLY LIKE: _____ (advertisement title)

	0%	25%	50%	75%	100%	
Numbers						
Words						TOTALS
Logic						
Lists						
Details						
Pictures						
Imagination						TOTALS
Colour						
Rhythm						
Space						

Figure 1.3 Sales Mind Matrix

Next do the same for the advertisement you selected that you don't like. Study the advertisement carefully and write in the title of the advertisement below for future reference. Now go through each of the ten mental skills in the same way as before, this time using the Sales Mind Matrix depicted in Figure 1.4.

DON'T LIKE: _____ (advertisement title)

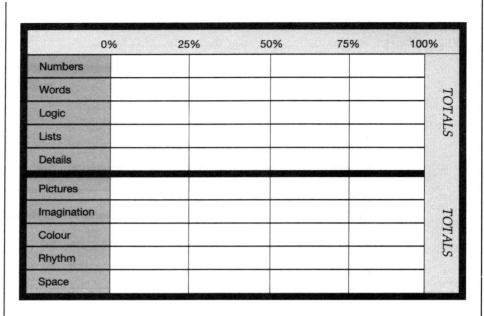

Figure 1.4   Sales Mind Matrix

Finally, compare your two Sales Mind Matrix profiles. What conclusions can you draw?

The truth-seeking brain

A profound discovery

One of the new realizations about the brain is that it *is* a truth-seeking mechanism. This is a discovery as profound as Newton's discovery of gravity. Gravity had always been there but it was Newton who first identified it, and Newton who had to explain the implications and ramifications of this new realization. It is now known that the brain needs truth. From birth, the brain is on a constant quest for truth, which is why children constantly demand that things be 'fair' and ask 'why?' Truth is accurate information.

If, for example, the brain does not know the truth that a 50-ton vehicle travelling at 80 miles per hour has certain effects on the human body when they make contact, then what will that brain do? Stand in front of that vehicle as the last conscious act of its life! In other words, the brain needs to know the truth to survive. The more accurate data it has in its mental data bank, the greater possibility not only of survival, but also of increasing success. It is for this reason that most people feel particularly uneasy when lying to others. On a deep and profound level, their own brain knows that, by lying, it is threatening its own survival and that of others.

A mutually rewarding relationship

The history of sales is littered with those who thought that bending the truth would lead to success. Instead, it generally results in failure and lack of self-confidence, and lack of respect for and from others. The great salespeople became great because, among other characteristics outlined in *Brain Sell*, they realized at an early stage in their careers that telling the truth was the finest service they could offer their customers. Telling the truth yields a satisfied customer, which in turn yields sales. This mutually rewarding relationship is one of the defining characteristics of a successful salesperson.

Performance that matches your potential?

Why is it that, despite the multimillions of pounds that have been spent on sales training, the results are so often disappointing? If you think back to the Sales Mind Matrix you will probably find the answers!

We took 35 sales books and manuals at random from our libraries and studied each one. Here's what we found. Each one covered the steps of the sale, which, in summary, appeared as:

- Step 1. Approach your customer.
- Step 2. Ask your customer questions.
- Step 3. Find out your customer's needs.
- Step 4. Make a presentation. Include benefit statements.
- Step 5. Overcome customer objections.
- Step 6. Close the sale.

The above sales steps are known as the basics to selling – basics which have been taught for the last 50 years. (For more details, see the Appendix, Sales Basics on page 65.) Look back at your Sales Mind Matrix on page 14 and decide whether these steps fit into the top box, the bottom box or both boxes in the Matrix? Next ask yourself, 'Do *all* sales pass through exactly these same six steps?' What about the customer who imagines using your product and simply says, 'I'll take it'? Did she miss steps one to five above?

We also noticed a considerable emphasis placed on 'closing techniques'. Indeed, some books dealt exclusively with these, whilst others stressed closing and answering objections. How do 'closing techniques' fit in with the customer's truth-seeking brain? Of course, there is a time and place to ask closing questions, but consider how your truth-seeking brain would react if closing techniques were used on you repeatedly.

Our belief is that something is not right! Customers are using both their truth-seeking brain as well as their Sales Mind Matrix when making a buying decision. You need to consider this and keep asking yourself 'Am I telling the truth?' and 'Am I using all of the Sales Mind Matrix skills in my sales?'

For a sales medical check-up, take the following test. Answer with your truth-seeking brain.

Skill Builder 7: your sales career

Answer the following questions, by ticking (✓) your answer.

When at work:

		YES	NO
1.	Do you forget prices, products and services you are selling?		
2.	Have you found yourself bored recently?		
3.	Have you turned off customers?		
4.	Have you recently lost your temper?		
5.	Have you wanted to leave work early, without a good reason?		
6.	Have you been rude on the phone in the last few weeks?		
7.	Have your sales been poor lately?		
8.	Have you been angry for no apparent reason?		
9.	Do you wish you had a different job?		
10.	Do you dislike your boss?		

TOTAL SCORE

Analysis

Question 1:   If you are having trouble remembering, Part One, Chapter 3, 'Memory Imprints', will solve this for you.

Question 2:   Daydreaming/imagination is a natural and wonderful function of the brain. In Part Four, Chapter 10, 'Sales Focus', you will discover how the application of your imagination makes work both interesting and exciting.

Question 3:   Once you have mastered 'Insight', (Part Two, Chapter 6), you will have customers wanting to be with you!

Question 4:   Controlling your temper will be easy once you understand the mind–body link found in Part Two, Chapter 6 'Insight'.

Question 5:   Why be absent when you enjoy working and meeting new people? Once you become a sales detective you will love every minute of selling. See 'Sales Detective' (Part Three, Chapter 8 has the answers).

Question 6:   Your telephone techniques will become fresh and exciting once you know how to make a memorable sales call. Study 'Power Hooks' (Part Four, Chapter 11), to ensure that you do!

Question 7:   Poor sales will become a distant memory once you understand what customers want as explained in 'The Sales Compass' (Part Three, Chapter 9).

Question 8:   Being angry is a sure sign of stress. You will have stress under control once you get to the stress reduction techniques in 'Insight' (Part Two, Chapter 6).

Question 9:   You will have the job of your dreams when you discover who you really are in 'SuperSellf' (Part Four, Chapter 12).

Question 10: Getting along with your boss, or anyone else will be easy once you have people regarding you as 'The Expert'. Study and master 'Infocentre' (Part Two, Chapter 4), and you will be surprised at your popularity!

Review

The good news is that your brain wants you to be a success, to be happy, and to have a satisfying job. Your brain is a success mechanism. If up to now you have been feeding it rubbish, then the results will have been yet more rubbish for your brain works on the formula, 'rubbish in, rubbish grows'. Of course, this formula can be changed just as easily to 'success in, success grows'. There are two quick ways to do this:

1   Use your truth-seeking brain.
2   Use your Sales Mind Matrix

The Sales Mind Matrix and the truth-seeking brain are the foundations to *Brain Sell*. Each chapter adds strength and emphasis to this basic framework. You need to keep asking yourself if you are using all aspects of the Sales Mind Matrix in your daily work. As you use the Sales Mind Matrix as a check and reference, you will become more aware and conscious of its power and application to your every sales activity.

As you listen to other sales presentations, as well as your own, ask your truth-seeking brain if it is pleased with what it's hearing.

Keep practising and applying the Sales Mind Matrix and the multiplier effect on your life in both improved quality and successes will astound you. The next chapter adds a new dimension to the Sales Mind Matrix: multisensory communication.

Skill Builder 8: whole-brain selling review

On a separate piece of blank paper, summarize this chapter, 'Whole-brain selling'. You may look back.

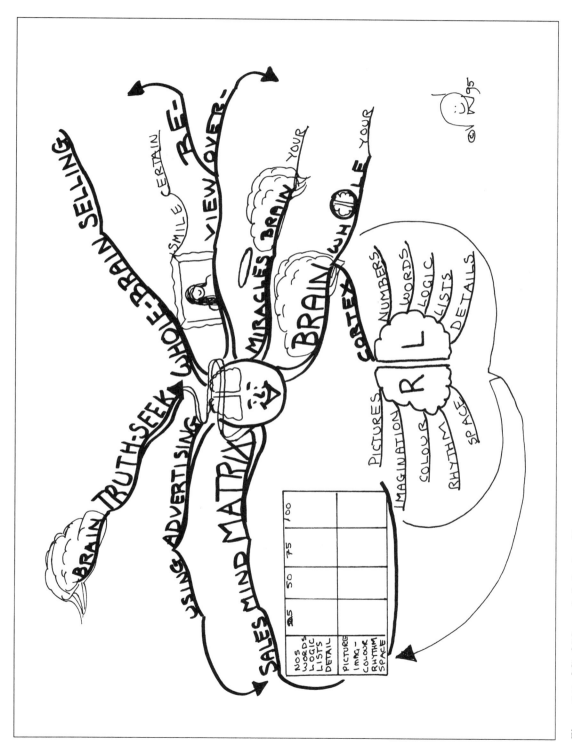

Figure 1.5 Mind Map: whole-brain selling

2　Salesenses

Make your senses sell

The hidden switch

Imagine that you own a transistor radio that you have played for years. One day you find a small switch on the back of your radio. You push the switch and up comes a range of new stations, ones you never heard before, from far-off lands, in different languages! You realize that the hidden switch activates the short wave function, enabling you to tune in to a new world.

Next, imagine finding a similar switch in your own 'bio computer', your brain! When you turn it on, you observe a change in how you send and receive information. This magic switch starts your multisensory information system.

This gives you the advantage that all the information you collect, store and retrieve is in a new dimension. The brain now uses all its senses to give a three-dimensional movie effect. Just think how easy it will be to remember and retrieve any information you want, and how this will benefit both you and your customers!

And all you have to do is turn the switch...

Overview

In this chapter you discover *the last four feet*, the physical distance between you and your customer and the arena in which sales are either made or lost. You will learn how information enters your brain in a sensory format and how to improve the way you communicate, enriching every aspect of your life, by using salesenses selling techniques.

The last four feet

The last four feet is that all-important distance between the customer and the salesperson. We want you to think of this area as the critical arena of your sales performance – your work area. For an actor, it's the stage; for the athlete, it's the track; for the surgeon, it's the operating theatre; for the pilot, it's the cockpit; for the salesperson, it's *the last four feet*. This could apply to face-to-face selling, a sales brochure, an advertisement, a billboard – anywhere that your sales message comes into contact with your customer.

Imagine that you are seated in a plane at London's Heathrow Airport, waiting for the pilot to appear. He is 20 minutes late and apologizes, explaining that he went to a party last night, had too much to drink and overslept this morning. He says he will get you to Rome on time by flying a little faster. But you are flying to Paris! How would you feel in this situation? Would you believe that the pilot is competent to handle the plane's controls in the cockpit, his *last four feet*.

Your journey

You must take *the last four feet* seriously. Each time you enter this critical area you are conducting your life's work, earning wealth and being of service. It is where you are focused and alert and where your truth-seeking brain is functioning at its best. It is the area which the salesperson must enter daily and use the Sales Mind Matrix. It's an area of endless learning – a classroom. It is the space where you gain and apply all your knowledge of selling.

How many salespeople are truly ready to enter *the last four feet*? Next time you go shopping, observe the salespeople. Are they attentive, informed, truthful and pleased to serve you? Or are they tired, un-interested, gum-chewing, bad-mannered, poorly dressed, half-asleep, mumbling, poorly informed, talking to friends on the phone and wish you would disappear? Are they ready to enter *the last four feet*?

The customer's journey

For the customer, *the last four feet* is an important area too. It is the end of the journey: from reading the advertisement; thinking about visiting you;

making the journey; walking in; and arriving with all the promises of a great experience and with high expectations of an enjoyable transaction. What happens between the salesperson and the customer in those magic four feet is the reason for this book.

Put your best foot forward

When you enter *the last four feet,* you need to be at your intellectual best – in a state of excellence. Many salespeople are victims of their moods. On a good day, they feel more energetic and do a better job of selling. But when they feel depressed, they may drag themselves to work and lack the enthusiasm needed to sell successfully.

The authors' life work involves the study of thousands of sales transactions, interviewing and observing some of the world's top sales talents, researching the brain, the great brains and the creative brains (see Tony Buzan's *Book of Genius*). You can apply our knowledge to what happens in those last four feet to turn your sales career into an exciting and rewarding top performance masterpiece.

At Perimeter Mall in Atlanta, Richard designed and installed a selling skills programme known as 'The Power Is Within You'. One participant was Valerie Gutknecht the manager of a ladies sportswear store called Khakis. A top sales producer, Gutknecht was always smiling, bubbling and leading her front line on to higher sales. It was no surprise to find a Teddy Bear permanently perched in the front window of her store, her head office's way of recognizing the store with the highest sales for that month.

Enthusiasm, like all emotions, is contagious. If you are smiling, relaxed and energetic, your customers will sense it. More importantly, customers will remember a salesperson who makes them feel good.

Skill Builder 9: a state of excellence

You can train yourself to be enthusiastic and to fight off those feelings of depression that so damage your sales performance. Here is a simple way to achieve a state of excellence by developing your own safe anchor.

First, choose a part of your body, such as your wrist, upper arm or shoulder that can be touched in public whenever you wish. Next, find a place where you can relax and not be disturbed. Let your mind drift back to when you did something very well. Remember what you saw then. Remember what you heard. Lastly, remember how you felt. Each time you remember something you did very well, touch or squeeze the chosen part of your body.

After completing this exercise, you will be able to recall powerful positive feelings at any time, simply by touching or squeezing that spot – that anchor.

A variation on this exercise is to assign a special word to that experience and then use the special word to call up the memory. Or you can use both touch and the special word to give yourself an extra link. Practise this exercise twice more to ensure that the touch or your chosen special word immediately recalls the memory of doing something very well. You can make this memory even more powerful by adding to it each time you have a sales success. In the future, when you make a sale and you feel really good, touch the spot or say the special word and strengthen the anchoring memory. Apply this technique every time you enter *the last four feet* so that you will be in a state of excellence, ready to be your best.

Senses selling

Let's start understanding your brain by studying how it takes in information from its surroundings. Have you considered the different ways in which you receive information? So many of us think that reading and talking are the only two ways information is received and stored by the brain, but that is not the case.

- *Sound*: You hear language used to express ideas, answer questions and persuade. The voice, speed, tone, and pitch of the words make hearing the spoken word a powerful experience.
- *Sight*: You rely heavily on your eyes for communications. Visual communication is a very influential method of sending information and takes many forms. Up to 85 per cent of the information we accept is through the eyes, making sight the most important sensory instrument we have.
- *Smell*: Next time you walk through the cosmetic department in a department store, chances are that some salesperson will approach you and offer to spray you with a line of perfume or aftershave! Why? Because, cosmetic companies know that your brain will remember the fragrance long after you've forgotten any sales talk or pretty packaging.
- *Taste*: All those taste buds on your tongue communicate to your brain. If you walked through your supermarket and a company was supply-

ing samples of a new cheese, wouldn't you be tempted to taste it? Manufacturers use this technique constantly. Just think how powerful the memory of taste is when you find a new flavour to enjoy!

- *Touch*: You are in a clothing store and find a garment you like. Would you touch the fabric to make sure that the fabric feels good against your skin? Touch is a powerful method of communication.

Information can be communicated using all five senses or a combination of any of the five. The more you can use all the senses or a combination of the senses, the stronger the communication. Think back to how you used your senses in Skill Builder 9, 'A state of excellence', page 31.

Skill Builder 10: sense check – a taste of chocolate

The following exercises help you to develop the use of your sale-senses, using a situation in which a salesperson is selling chocolate to a customer. After reading the exchange of the conversation, you will receive further instructions.

The scene takes place in a speciality store that sells only chocolate. Hundreds of bars of all types and sizes from throughout the world are on display. The store is bright and attractive, permeated with the sound of pleasant background music and delicious aromas. We listen in to the conversation between the customer and the salesperson ...

Salesperson: 'You mentioned that you wanted a rich, dark chocolate, with nuts.'
Customer: 'Yes, that's right.'
Salesperson: 'Here, taste this. It has a dark chocolate taste. Notice its rich creamy texture, and it doesn't melt on your fingers. That chocolate smells delicious, and it comes in attractive heart shapes. What do you think?'
Customer: 'Hmm, it's good.'

Instructions

Read the conversation again. Next to each of the customer's five senses listed below, write down which, if any, of the customer's senses, were appealed to, using examples from the above dialogue. The item is dark chocolate. Then check your answers against the list overleaf:

- *Sound*:

- *Sight*:

- *Smell*:

- *Taste*:

- *Touch*:

Suggested answers:

- *Sound*: The customer hears the spoken, sensory words used by the salesperson.
- *Sight*: '...it comes in attractive heart shapes.' The salesperson attracts the customer's *eyes* to the heart design.
- *Smell*: 'That chocolate smells delicious ...'. The salesperson directs the customer's sense of *smell* to the product.
- *Taste*: 'Here, taste this. It has a dark chocolate taste.' The salesperson draws the customer's attention to the *taste*.
- *Touch*: 'Notice its rich creamy texture, and it doesn't melt on your fingers.' The salesperson is encouraging the customer to *feel* the chocolate to confirm the fact that it does not melt on the fingers.

Evidently, our salesperson did an excellent job in appealing to all her customer's senses. How did you do in deciding what senses the salesperson used?

Skill Builder 11: the feel of a Jaguar

How about another try? Here, a car salesperson is taking a customer for a demonstration ride in a new car. First, study the following.

The customer is test-driving a new Jaguar, with the salesperson as the passenger. The road is clear, the weather is dry and sunny and the radio is playing softly in the background. We listen in to their conversation …

Salesperson: 'Notice how smooth the ride is. You can taste the luxury. Feel the deep padded, leather seats – it almost feels as though you're floating doesn't it? Can you smell that new leather?'
Customer: 'Yes.'
Salesperson: 'Look, the new digital panel shows that we are now up to 55 miles per hour, and the engine is as quiet as a mouse. How about that?'
Customer: 'Not bad!'

Now read the conversation again. Next to each of the customer's five senses listed below, write down what, if any, of the customer's senses were appealed to, using examples from the dialogue. The item is a 'new car'. Check your answers against the section below.

- *Sound*:

- *Sight*:

- *Smell*:

- *Taste*:

- *Touch*:

Suggested answers:

- *Sound*: '…the engine is as quiet as a mouse.' The salesperson draws the customer's attention to the *sound* of the engine.
- *Sight*: 'Look, the new digital panel shows that we are now up to 55 miles per hour …'. The salesperson attracts the customer's *eyes* to the instrument panel to confirm the speed.
- *Smell*: 'Can you smell that new leather?' The salesperson is directing the customer's sense of *smell*.
- *Taste*: 'You can taste the luxury.' The salesperson conjures up the *taste* of luxury.
- *Touch*: 'Feel the deep padded, leather seats – it almost feels as though you're floating …'. The salesperson is encouraging the customer to *feel* the leather seats.

Again, our salesperson did an excellent job in stimulating his customer's senses.

Skill Builder 12: a nose for cleaning

You can use senses in selling a service just as easily. In this exercise, a salesperson is selling dry cleaning to a customer. Study the conversation, follow the instructions, then check your answers against the section below.

The scene is a dry cleaners. The premises are neat and shiny in appearance, and you can see all the equipment and people working in the background. The customer is discussing her blouse with the salesperson. We listen to their conversation …

Customer: 'Can you get this stain out?'
Salesperson: 'Yes, of course we can – we have a special treatment that will make your blouse look as good as new. When you get it back, you'll see the original colour and you'll feel the silky texture. There's no chemical after-smell with this treatment. It's really good.'

Instructions

Read the conversation again. Next to each of the customer's senses listed below, write down which, if any, of the customer's senses were appealed to, using examples from the above dialogue. The item was 'dry cleaning'.

- *Sound*:

- *Sight*:

- *Smell*:

- *Taste*:

- *Touch*:

Suggested answers:

- *Sound*: The salesperson used *spoken, sensory words* to conduct the conversation.
- *Sight*: 'Your blouse will look as good as new …' and '… you'll see the original colour …'. Our salesperson has directed her customer's *sight* twice to the blouse.
- *Smell*: 'There's no chemical after-smell with this treatment …'. Here the salesperson appeals to the customer's sense of *smell*.
- *Taste*:
- *Touch*: 'You'll feel the silky texture.' The salesperson draws the customer's attention to the *feel* of the texture.

In three simple, uninterrupted sentences the salesperson appealed to four of the customer's five senses – sound, sight, smell and touch. Although it was only one small speech did you notice how powerful it was in building a complete picture? We term this technique 'salesenses' as it appeals to all the customer's senses by creating selling pictures. Remember, 'one picture is worth a thousand words'.

> You are an artist: your art is in your words. By skilfully choosing your words, you can create those sales pictures in your customer's mind.

Salesenses in action

To illustrate the application of salesenses let's first see what happens at most travel agencies and then apply our new *Brain Sell* technology to the situation.

It's 11 a.m. on a dreary Monday morning. You walk into a travel agency wanting information about holidays in Hawaii. The agent is on the phone. You take a seat. As the agent puts down the phone, it rings again and a long conversation ensues. Eventually, the agent asks you 'What do you have in mind?'

'A holiday in Hawaii,' you whisper back, afraid to interrupt.

'Over there. The brochures are over there,' says the agent, pointing to a wall of brochures, then continues talking on the phone, ignoring you.

Richard, working with a team of British Airways managers, came up with this salesenses result.

It's 11 a.m. on a dreary Monday morning. You walk into your travel agency and ask for information about holidays in Hawaii. You suddenly find yourself handed a Hawaiian shirt. Then, a garland is placed around your neck, you are offered a cool pineapple drink and told all about Waikiki Beach while soft guitar music plays in the background. When you've finished drinking, the agent asks 'When would you like to go?'

'How about now!' you reply.

A sales presentation which taps into each of the five senses – sound, sight, smell, taste and touch – is extremely powerful. This is one of the great secrets of selling success: customers need to picture themselves using your product and service before they are ready to buy.

Advertisers successfully use this technique. Every time you see a television commercial, a magazine advertisement or a billboard poster, your mind is soaking up images and pictures of the advertised product.

The complete Sales Mind Matrix

In Chapter 1, you were introduced to the ten mental skills that make up the Sales Mind Matrix-1. In this chapter, you have been introduced to the five salesenses. The complete Sales Mind Matrix blends the ten mental skills and the five salesenses. The complete Sales Mind Matrix is illustrated below.

	0%	25%	50%	75%	100%	
Sound						TOTALS
Sight						
Smell						
Taste						
Touch						
Numbers						TOTALS
Words						
Logic						
Lists						
Details						
Pictures						TOTALS
Imagination						
Colour						
Rhythm						
Space						

Figure 2.1   Sales Mind Matrix – complete

Fill in the complete Sales Mind Matrix as you did on page 14, but this time include your five senses. Do you notice any changes from your first attempt? Which are your strongest and weakest senses?

Skill Builder 13: use your five senses

Think of a product or service you are selling. Next, think of ways you can explain your item to the customer using all five of the customer's senses in any creative way and write it in the appropriate spaces below.

*Item:*_____

- *Sound*:

- *Sight*:

- *Smell*:

- *Taste*:

- *Touch*:

You know now that the brain is a multisensory organ. It takes in information through your senses of sight, sound, smell, taste and touch. The more you learn to use all your senses, the easier it will be to use salesenses conversations.

Skill Builder 14: vivid impressions

Think back to your last big sale. (If you are not a salesperson think back to your last major purchase.) Read the following questions then write down your answers. What four things did you see when you got the order, then what four sounds did you hear, and what four sensations did you feel? If you cannot think of four answers, write down as many as you can.

- What did I *see* when I got the order?

    1.
    2.
    3.
    4.

- What did I *hear* when I got the order?

    1.
    2.
    3.
    4.

- What did I *feel* when I got the order?

    1.
    2.
    3.
    4.

You can now add the above answers to strengthen your anchor, your state of excellence (Skill Builder 9, page 31).

Review

In this chapter we have taken a fresh look at the whole brain, both the customer's and the salesperson's. We now have a new understanding of how information is collected by the five senses, stored and retrieved. All this happens between a customer and a salesperson in *the last four feet*, the physical distance between the two. This important area is where the salesperson must be at his best, in a state of excellence.

You have found the switch that turns on a new part of your brain, a part that has been dormant for years, waiting to be switched on. You can now progress to sell, using all your senses. Your life is taking on an exciting new dimension as you see, hear and feel the potential of what lies ahead.

You are becoming an excellent communicator: by using salesenses you have taken your first important step. Using your Sales Mind Matrix, your truth-seeking brain and your salesenses, you are now ready to move on to the next chapter and master the subject most requested by salespeople worldwide.

Skill Builder 15: salesenses review

On a separate piece of blank paper, summarize this chapter, 'Salesenses'. You may look back.

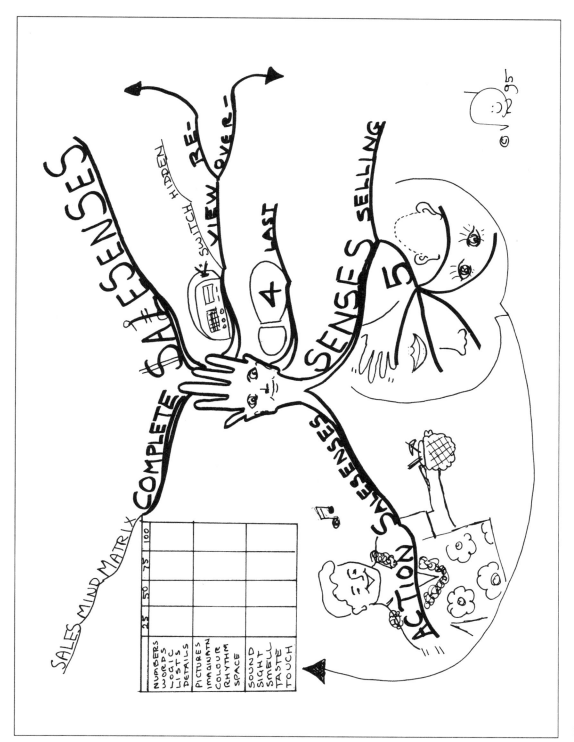

Figure 2.2 Mind Map: salesenses

3   Memory imprints

I remember YOU!

Become instantly likeable

Imagine from this moment on that every customer you meet takes an instant liking to you. More importantly, as time goes by, your customers like you more and more. Customers are now calling to ask your advice, ordering from you over the phone and recommending their friends to buy from you!

Somehow you have made your way into your customers' minds and activated their brains so they can't forget you! Just think how much easier and how much more fun your job would be! To become instantly memorable, read, understand and practise everything in this chapter.

Overview

This chapter shows you how your Sales Mind Matrix can help you improve your sales memory. Memory improvement – specifically, how to remember customers' names and faces – is the subject most requested by salespeople worldwide. The Buzan Sales Manners Method takes you through a step-by-step process to the mastery of this important topic. Memory imprints will help you remember your customers and help your customers remember you.

Remembering names and faces

You must use your full Sales Mind Matrix to move into Chapter 3 which deals with how to make a favourable impression on your customer. This step covers the first visual and verbal contact you make in greeting or acknowledgment. The essential issue is how to get your customer's name and, once you have the name, to continue to use it throughout the sales conversation. This way you build a stronger bond in those last four feet. However, few salespeople who obtain their customer's name at the beginning of the sales conversation can remember and use the customer's name throughout the conversation and at future meetings!

Why is remembering customers' names and faces one of the more difficult aspects of the sale? The reason for the difficulty lies in the fact that most names have no 'connection' to the faces. In earlier times it was exactly the opposite; the whole system helped you remember. Names and faces were based on memory and association: the man you regularly saw covered in white flour with dough in his hands was Mr Baker. As time passed, the family name became increasingly removed from its initial meaning, making the task of memorizing names and faces increasingly difficult. Nowadays a person's name rarely has an immediate association with his face or demeanour.

There are two principal methods of mastering this skill, each method supporting the other. The first is the Buzan Sales Manners Method and the second, the Sales Memory Method.

The Buzan Sales Manners Method

The Buzan Sales Manners Method for remembering names and faces promises that you will remember all your future customers' names the first time you hear them. It requires two simple things of you:

1. an interest in the people you meet;
2. politeness.

Many salespeople love to meet people; maybe that's why you chose this profession as opposed to working in an office! Meeting people is part of your job description. Enjoying meeting people is part of your job satisfaction and success. When you practise these techniques you will enjoy far greater self-confidence, more direct communication and improved sales performance.

The Buzan Sales Manners Method has 14 steps which ensure that you start your sale in the right direction, by activating your customer's brain and gaining his or her undivided attention.

Step 1: the mental set

Before you enter *the last four feet*, mentally prepare to succeed. Salespeople who believe they are bad at remembering names and faces continually prove it to themselves! If you 'know' that your sales memory will improve, you will notice an immediate improvement. When preparing yourself for *the last four feet*, make sure that you are as poised, alert and confident as possible, and that you are mentally prepared. Regard your sales memory as a favourite hobby and bring to it all the enthusiasm and energy you would put into it.

Step 2: observe

As you enter *the last four feet*, look your customer straight in the eye. Don't shift your eyes around to the floor or ceiling. As you look at your customers' faces, note their particular facial characteristics, for this will help you in the memorization of names and faces.

Skill Builder 16: let's face it

In the frame below draw a face and list all its different characteristics (for example, eyes, nose etc.).

Below is a guided tour from the top of the head to the tip of the chin, with many tips on how to classify the features. This will help you to see more clearly, define more individually and uniquely, remember better and store better. When you look at your customer's head, look for each one of the following characteristics first for its complete structure and then for some specific and particular unique things about it. For example, we have a friend who has very little hair left and has a happy rounded face. His name is Mike Merryspoon and we remember him because he is happy, or merry, and his bald head reminds us of the smooth surface of a spoon, so we have the connection 'Merryspoon'. Here, we have used association.

Head

In *the last four feet*, you first meet a customer's head. Heads come in three general sizes: large; medium; and small. Within these sizes are various shapes: square; rectangular; oval; broad; narrow; round; flat at the front; flat on top; flat at the back; domed at the back; face angled with jutting chin and slanted forehead; or face angled with receding chin and prominent forehead.

Hair

Because, in earlier times, people kept the same hairstyle they served as better memory hooks than they do now. Nevertheless, some basic characteristics can be listed as follows:

- *Men*: thick; fine; wavy; straight; parted; receding; bald; cropped; medium-length; long; frizzy; colour.
- *Women*: thick, thin; fine. Because of the variety and constant change in women's hairstyles and colours it is unwise to use these features as a principal memory hook.

Forehead

Foreheads can be generally divided into the following types: high; wide; narrow between hairline and eyebrows; narrow between temples; smooth; lined horizontally; lined vertically.

Eyebrows

Eyebrows may be: thick; thin; long; short; meeting at the middle; spaced apart; flat; arched; winged; bushy; tapered.

Eyelashes

These may be: thick; thin; long; short; curled; straight.

Eyes

Eyes may be: large; small; protruding; deep-set; close together; spaced apart; slanted outward; slanted inwards; coloured; whole iris visible; iris covered partly by either or both of the upper or lower lids. The upper and lower lids may be large or small, smooth or wrinkled, puffy or firm.

Nose

When seen from the front the nose may be: large; small; narrow; medium; wide; crooked. When seen in profile it may be: straight; flat; pointed; blunt; snub or upturned; Roman or aquiline; Greek, forming a straight line with forehead; concave (caved in). The base of the nose can also vary considerably in relation to the nostrils, being: lower; level; a little higher. The nostrils themselves can also vary: straight; curved downwards; flaring; wide; narrow; hairy.

Cheekbones

Cheekbones are often linked very closely with other facial characteristics when viewed from the front, but the following four characteristics are often worth noting: high; low; regular; obscured.

Ears

Few salespeople pay attention to ears, yet their individuality can be greater than any other feature. They may be: large; small; gnarled; smooth; round; oblong; triangular; flat against the head; protruding; hairy; large-lobed; unlobed; uneven. Men's ears are usually easier to remember, as women often have their ears covered by their hair.

Lips

Lips vary in the following ways: thick upper lip; thin upper lip; small; thick; wide; thin; upturned; downturned; Cupid's bow; well shaped; ill-defined.

Chin

When viewed straight-on, the chin may be: long; short; pointed; square; round; double (or multiple); cleft; dimpled. When seen from the side, it may be: jutting; straight; double (or multiple); receding.

Skin

Skin may be: smooth; rough; dark; fair; blemished or marked in some way; oily; dry; blotchy; doughy; wrinkled; furrowed; coloured or suntanned; freckled.

Make a hobby of remembering names and faces. It is a known fact that when you engage in a hobby your observational powers and sales memory dramatically improve!

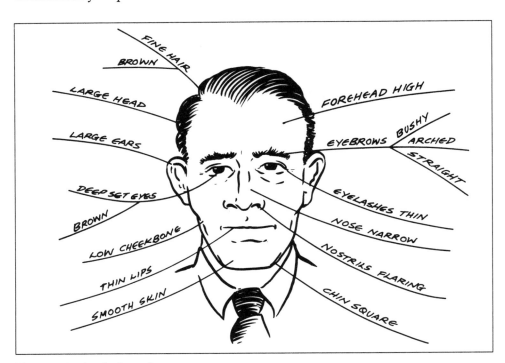

Figure 3.1   Analysing a face

Mindless looking, instead of true observation, is one of the principal causes of poor memory. You can programme your mind to observe this by 'exercising' your observational powers with each one of your customers. For example, one day concentrate on noses, another day eyebrows, another day ears, and so on. You will find, to your surprise, that each part of each face varies enormously from customer to customer, and that your increasing observation of the differences will help you remember the faces of the new customers that you meet.

Step 3: listen

Consciously listen, paying attention to the sound of the new customer's name. Many salespeople are so concerned with what they intend to say next that they either do not hear, or pay the necessary attention to the customer's name at this important stage. Listen with the intentness of someone who is 'hard of hearing'.

Step 4: repeat

When you have heard the customer's name, repeat it. This ensures that you have pronounced it correctly, gives the customer a chance to correct the pronunciation, if wrong, and shows him or her that you were listening.

Imagine a customer walking up and entering *the last four feet*. You, the salesperson, make eye contact and smile as you prepare to start the sales conversation. As you introduce yourself, you ask for your customer's name.

Salesperson: 'My name is Meadow, as in the cows in the meadow' (*laughing*).

You have now made it easy for your customer to remember your name through association and your laughter has relaxed your customer, enabling you to continue as demonstrated below.

Salesperson: 'And what is your name?'
Customer: 'Cleveland.'
Salesperson: '*Cleveland*?'
Customer: 'Yes, that's right.'

Now you have the customer's name and you have repeated it. This shows that you were listening, interested, have remembered it and are now ready to continue. Repetition is an important memory aid: each repetition of any item you wish to learn greatly increases your ability to remember it.

Step 5: request the spelling

If there is any doubt about the spelling of the name, politely or playfully ask the customer for the spelling, again confirming your interest and allowing another natural repetition of the name. For example:

Salesperson: 'Mrs Hugenot…that's an unusual name. May I ask how you spell it?'
Customer: 'Why, H-U-G-E-N-O-T.'
Salesperson: 'I've got it. H-U-G-E-N-O-T.'

Step 6: discuss

To enhance your new hobby discover the derivation of names. You will find that this not only makes the remembering of names and faces a delight but it also opens worlds of new knowledge and friendship to you.

On hearing the customer's name, explain to him or her that you have a great interest in the background and derivation of names and politely ask if she or he knows anything about the history of the family name. (However, be sure that you know the history of your own name!) It might surprise you to know that, on average, 60 per cent of your customers know some background to their name and are enthusiastic about discussing it. Provided you have sufficient time, this technique gives a great opportunity to establish immediate contact and build a rapport with the customer.

Step 7: swap memory cards

The Japanese have developed the practice of card-exchange into a major element of their social etiquette, realizing how useful it is for sales memory. Following their example, whenever possible, ask for the customer's business card. Not only does this give you the correct spelling and address for future sales correspondence and sales mailing lists, it also enables you to write brief sales notes on the back. For example, if you find yourself selling at a trade show where you might meet a few hundred people in a day, writing little sales notes on the back of the customers' business cards will prove invaluable when reviewing the cards and deciding what sales follow-up action is needed. You should always have your business card available to make it easier for your customer to remember you and be able to contact you for future sales transactions.

Step 8: repeat aloud

Keep using your customer's name, within reason, throughout the sales conversation. Not only does this repetition help implant the customer's name more firmly in your memory, but each time you use it you gain and hold his attention and demonstrate that you have remembered his name. People love to hear their name.

Step 9: brain spell

During any pause in the sales conversation, repeat the customer's name to yourself. You will find that this makes the name second nature to you. Better still, with your eyes open, create your customer's name on your internal video screen. Make the letters large, put them in colour, emphasize the correct spelling, move the letters around, and make them brighter. This Brain Spell method is a highly effective way to remember names. Stop reading for a few moments and try this technique with your own name!

Step 10: repeat at parting

As you close the sales conversation, always make certain that you use the customer's name. As you will learn later (Part Four, Chapter 11, 'Power Hooks'), the start and the ending of the sales conversation are two of the essential and memorable stages of the sale from the customer's point of view. By including their names in these sections of the conversation, you are strengthening your link with your customers.

Step 11: mentally review

Take a moment to think about your favourite customer. Did you get a name or mental picture when you thought of that customer? Chances are that you did. Now, consider what you did mentally to remember that favourite customer – in other words, conduct a mental review. Subsequently, each time you do this, you will strengthen the sales memory of that customer in your mind. Here is a big sales memory tip: *if you want to remember that customer, keep mentally reviewing him or her at least once a day for 7 days.* This 7-day mental review allows the long-term memory to capture all the data.

When you have parted from your new customer, quickly flash on your internal video screen his or her name, face, purchase and any other details you wish to remember. Do this by creating, in your mind, a central image of the customer and then adding details of names, associations, purchases and so on. (We will cover this technique in more detail in Part Three.) When you have the odd spare moment during your sales day, practise the mental review of your customers. You will be surprised at how much you can remember, and in what detail, as you develop this new mental sales skill.

Step 12: reverse the process

Whenever possible, reverse the process through which you have just been with your customer. For example, when you introduce yourself to your customer, repeat your own name and give the spelling and, if it seems appropriate, even its background. Maybe there is some link between your name and another item which will help your customer remember your name. If you have a business card make certain that you present it. Throughout the conversation, if you are referring to yourself, use your own name. For example, instead of saying 'My husband asked me about this the other day', say 'My husband said, "Joan, how long have we had this…?"'. This will help your customer remember and use your name during the sales conversation. Besides, being more polite, it makes the sales conversation more personal, enjoyable and friendly.

Step 13: pace yourself

There is a tendency, because of the stress in *the last four feet*, to rush through the introduction. The most successful salespeople take time to memorize their customers' names and faces at the beginning of the sale.

Step 14: have fun

If you make the learning of names and faces an enjoyable and a serious game, the right hemisphere of your brain will feel far freer and open to make the imaginative associations and connections necessary to good memory. Children have better memories for names and faces than adults, not because their minds are superior but simply because they naturally apply all the principles outlined in this section.

Tony Buzan developed this method of remembering names and faces, based on the Sales Mind Matrix. You will be delighted how fast, effective and fun this method is, once you start to use it.

The Sales Memory Method

The Sales Memory Method involves remembering names and faces and adding details of your customers' purchases, interests, hobbies, preferences and family details. To understand how this works, we need a quick history into the principles of superpower memory.

The Greeks made a goddess out of memory – Mnemosyne – because they worshipped memory. The Greeks had worked this out for themselves by understanding the mental functions of what we now know as the Sales Mind Matrix. They had intuitively recognized three underlying principles that ensure perfect memory:

- imagination
- association
- motivation.

If you want to remember anything, all you have to do is to use your *imagination* to *associate* (link) it with some known or fixed item with a high level of *motivation* to ensure success.

The 'SMASHIN' SCOPE' of memory

The principles of perfect memory established by the Greeks fit exactly with the Sales Mind Matrix which we covered in the first two chapters. The Greeks realized that, to remember well, you have to use every aspect of your mind. Let's outline these principles. To have a powerful memory you must include in your mental pictures the following:

1. *Synaesthesia/sensuality*: Synaesthesia refers to the blending of the senses. Chapter 2, 'Salesenses', contained exercises to develop your sense of sight, sound, taste, touch and smell.
2. *Movement*: If you add movement to the image you wish to remember, it adds a further extensive range of possible 'links' for your brain. For example, you could make the image three-dimensional, then add music and rhythm. The more vivid the picture, the easier it is to remember. Try if for yourself. Imagine you are a child visiting the circus for the first time. The band starts to play a marching tune, as the huge African elephants, flicking their ears and tails, sway into the arena, their large feet moving in rhythm to the music. One walks past you; watch as the trunk moves towards you and then swings away. Close your eyes now, hear the music, see the picture and feel the excitement.

3. *Association*: Whatever you wish to memorize, make sure that you associate or link it to something stable in your mental environment. For example, if you own a car, then anything that moves can be linked to it. You could put your dancing elephant on to the roof of the car.
4. *Sexuality*: We all have a good memory in this area. Use it.
5. *Humour*: The funnier you make your images, the more outstanding and memorable they will be. Put your elephant in pink tights! Have fun with your memory.
6. *Imagination*: This is the powerhouse of your brain. The more you apply your vivid imagination to memory, the better your memory will become. Imagine your elephant sitting upon the car playing the saxophone with President Bill Clinton!
7. *Number*: Numbering makes the image more specific and efficient to remember. It provides order and structure and allows you to 'place' things in your infinite memory filing systems so that they are easily accessible and therefore recallable.
8. *Symbolism*: A symbol or meaningful image helps in recall. Consider a roadway 'stop' sign. How clear is that in your mind?
9. *Colour*: Whenever you can, add as many different colours as possible to your ideas and images. Colour aids memory. That 'stop' sign symbol – what colour is it?
10. *Order and sequence*: In combination with the other principles, order and sequence allow faster recall. Examples could be grouping by colour, moving from small to large or sorting by category. Imagine that all the male elephants in the circus are white and the female elephants are blue!
11. *Positive images*: Usually, positive and pleasant images will be remembered better because the brain likes to return to them. Think of your favourite foods!
12. *Exaggeration*: In your images exaggerate size, shape and sound to improve your ability to memorize them. Think of your white dancing elephant, on top of the car, playing the saxophone with President Clinton. Now double the size of your elephant, and make the music louder.

Now memorize these basic memory principles using the acronym 'SMASHIN' SCOPE'. This confirms the 'smashin' scope' of your limitless memory.

The following example demonstrates how this technique can be put effortlessly into use.

You have an important client, Bill Stanley, whom you have invited out to a business lunch. Bill and his wife Mary have two children, Mark and

Mandy. You know that Bill plays golf and enjoys salmon fishing. Mary plays tennis and paints. They have a cat, Walnut, and a dog Max. During the course of the lunch you intend to include the above in the conversation. You can't take out a notebook at the dinner table to look up the information, so you use SMASHIN' SCOPE to remember it.

You form a picture of Mary painting a huge picture high on a wall using a tennis racket instead of a paint brush. To reach her picture Mary is standing on the shoulders of Mandy who in turn is standing on the shoulders of Mark whose legs are wobbling due to the weight. Both Mary, Mark and Mandy are wearing white T-shirts with a red letter M on the front, representing the first letter of their respective names. The picture which Mary is painting is unusual in that it's three-dimensional and moving. It's a picture of a gushing river. The cold water is spilling out of the frame and wetting your face! Bill is in the middle of the river, salmon fishing with his golf club. He catches a salmon and tosses it to the embankment where Walnut the cat is sleeping on a pile of giant walnuts. Max, the dog, is sitting on the grass drinking a cup of Maxwell House coffee.

This image is created using synaesthesia, movement, humour, imagination, numbers, colour, positive images and exaggeration. Close your eyes and see it. How easy would it now be to discuss all the different topics at lunch with Bill Stanley?

Summary

1. Confirm that you have a clear mental image of the customer's name.
2. Verify you can 'hear again' the sound of the customer's name by repeating the name of your customer in your mind.
3. Very carefully examine your customer's face, noting all its characteristics.
4. Look for unusual, distinct, extraordinary or unique facial characteristics.
5. Mentally reconstruct the customer's face, using your imagination as a cartoonist does to exaggerate any noteworthy features.
6. Associate, using your imagination, exaggeration and the general memory principles, any of the outstanding features with the name of the customer. For example, a customer with the name 'Wood' who is very tall could be associated with a tall tree.

Figure 3.2   Names and faces

Skill Builder 17: who is that?

Look closely at the faces in Figure 3.2, find characteristics that you could imaginatively associate with the name, repeat the name, and then make your memory image.

Use the principles outlined earlier to remember the customer's names associated with the faces. Look at each face carefully and remember as many as you can.

Write your answers in Figure 3.3 on page 61. Then check your answers against the original illustration.

Skill Builder 18: the Buzan Sales Manners Method

List below in correct order, and without looking back, the steps of the Buzan Sales Manners Method.

Skill Builder 19: SMASHIN' SCOPE

Without looking back, what does 'SMASHIN' SCOPE' stand for?

Skill Builder 20: secret to a magnificent memory

What is the secret of a magnificent memory?

Find the answers to the Skill Builders 18–20 on page 62.

Figure 3.3 Faces

Review

In this chapter we have covered two methods on how to make a lasting imprint in our customer's mind. As soon as you enter those last four feet, discover, and use, your customer's name.

The first method we covered was the Buzan Sales Manners Method. This method requires two simple things of you.

1.   Take an interest in the people you meet.
2.   Be polite.

We then took you through the 14 steps that make up this method. These were:

1.   The mental set
2.   Observe
3.   Listen
4.   Repeat
5.   Request the spelling
6.   Discuss
7.   Swap memory cards
8.   Repeat aloud
9.   Brain Spell
10. Repeat at parting
11. Mentally review
12. Reverse the process
13. Pace yourself
14. Have fun

The second method, the Sales Memory Method involves remembering names and faces and adding details of your customers' purchases, interests, hobbies, preferences, and family. To do this well, you need to build up a superpower memory with the help of SMASHIN' SCOPE, which stands for:

1.   **S**ynaesthesia/sensuality
2.   **M**ovement
3.   **A**ssociation
4.   **S**exuality
5.   **H**umour
6.   **I**magination
7.   **N**umber

8. **S**ymbolism
9. **C**olour
10. **O**rder and sequence
11. **P**ositive images
12. **E**xaggeration.

The secret to a magnificent memory is... . Well, we posed that question to Dominic O'Brien, the first World Memory Champion. Dominic is remarkable in that he developed his memory skills over a short period of five years and that he was completely self-taught! Dominic's answer was 'Memory is like a muscle, the more you *practise* the stronger it becomes.'

Skill Builder 21: Memory imprints review

On a separate piece of blank paper, summarize this chapter, 'Memory Imprints'. You may look back – or test your memory first!

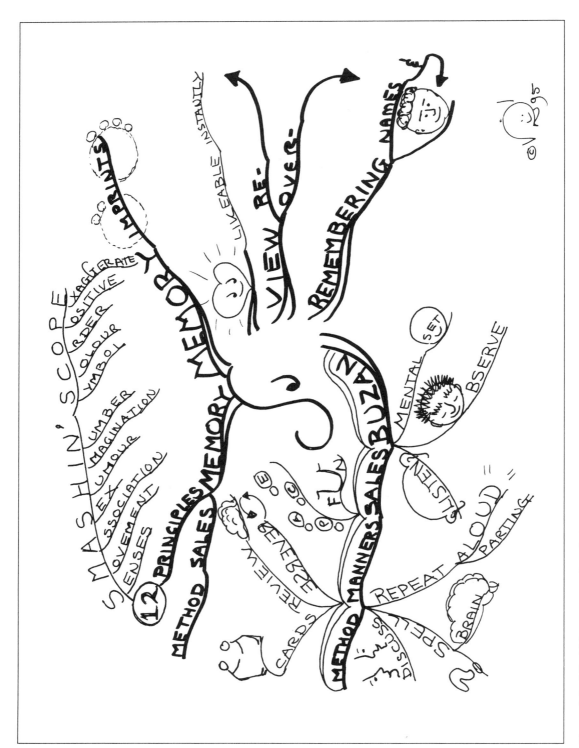

Figure 3.4 Mind Map: memory imprints

Appendix: sales basics

Since the 1940s sales training and sales techniques have been based on the work of E. K. Strong, known as the father of 'Benefit Selling'. He claims that sales move through a series of steps in which the salesperson first establishes the customer's needs, then sells features and benefits, overcomes the customer's objections and finally closes the sale.

Chances are that if you have been exposed to a sales training programme or read sales books in the last 50 years, this will sound familiar. We decided to include the techniques in *Brain Sell* for two reasons: first, to give a background to newcomers to the subject of selling; second, as a reminder to those who have previously been taught these techniques and wish to review them.

In 'Sales Basics' we will cover the five simple steps to a sale:

1. opening the sale;
2. establishing needs;
3. giving features, advantages and benefits;
4. handling objections;
5. closing techniques.

Opening the sale

In face-to-face selling, opening the sale is known as the approach. The objective here is to start a conversation in order to gain and hold the customer's attention. Emphasis is placed on making eye contact with the customer, smiling and asking open questions. Closed questions, such as 'Do you have life insurance?', can be answered with a simple 'Yes' or a 'No'. Open questions, as their name implies, encourage a more detailed answer and the opportunity to start a conversation. 'What would your family do without your income?' is an example of an open question.

Sales openings are categorized under a few classic titles.

- **The personal approach**. Here you need to know the customer's name and use it – for example, 'Hello, Mrs Grant. How is your new job working out for you?' The approach makes the customer feel special and lets her know that you recognized her. It also creates a friendly atmosphere.
- **The direct approach**. This approach goes straight to the point: 'Good afternoon, I wondered if you are interested in having your house painted?' This is the most common approach, and uses a closed question. If the customer's response is 'No', that could be the end of the matter!
- **The product or service approach**. Here, the name of the product or service you are selling is used in the opening sentence: 'I'm calling about our new model which is proving very popular.' It's commonly used in telephone selling or solicitations – for example, 'My name is O'Neil and I'm calling for Mothers Against Drunk Driving'. This approach is informative and focuses the customer's attention directly on the product or service being offered.
- **The opinion approach**. A clever approach is to get the customer both interested in the product or service and to express an opinion. On the phone this might be: 'Good morning Mr Edwards, we are conducting a survey on mutual funds and would like to ask you a few questions. Do you own a mutual fund?' In face-to-face selling, a customer who is examining an item might be approached and asked, 'Do you like this artist? She's new to our gallery and we wanted opinions on her work from customers.'

All the above approaches have one common aim – to start a conversation and to start building trust and rapport. You are probably using a similar approach yourself. After all, you have to say or do something to start the sale!

Establishing needs

Once you have started a sales conversation, the next stage is to establish the customer's needs for your product or service. This is done by observation. What is the customer showing interest in, touching, and examining? All of these are known as 'buying signals'. It is most important in this stage to ask qualifying questions designed to encourage customers to express their needs.

At BMW dealerships in South Africa, Richard trained salespeople to ask the following questions:

- 'What kind of car are you driving now?'
- 'How many miles do you drive a year?'
- 'How many are there in your family?'
- 'How much do you intend to spend?'
- 'Is boot space important?'
- 'Is this the first showroom you've come to?'
- 'Is this going to be a second car?'
- 'Was there anything special you were looking for in a car?'
- 'What colour do you prefer?'
- 'When do you need it?'

The answers to these questions give a fairly accurate picture of the car needed.

Giving features, advantages and benefits (FAB)

Now that you have the customer's needs, traditional sales training teaches you to present the appropriate features, advantages and benefits (FAB) of your product or service. This stage is also known as the sales presentation. In order to make the presentation and 'FAB' your product or service, you have to know your product knowledge and the appropriate FABs.

Product knowledge takes your product or service and breaks it down into its three component parts:

1. Features,
2. Advantages and
3. Benefits.

All products and services can be broken down into many features which in turn have both advantages and benefits, all of which answer a customer's expressed needs. This is known as 'Benefit Selling'. The following example, that Richard taught to Pye TV salespeople in England, explains the principle of FAB.

You decide to buy a new television as your picture quality is poor and you are tired of getting up from your chair to change channels. The salesperson, on hearing your expressed need, 'I am tired of getting up from the chair to change channels', introduces you to a television with a remote control stating, 'This remote control switches the set on and off, changes the channels and adjusts the volume. You can make these adjustments while relaxing in your chair.'

Features describe some characteristic of the product or service. If you ask the question, 'What is it?', the answer will always be a feature. In our example, the feature was a remote control.

Advantages explain what the features do. They answer the question, 'What does the feature do?'. In the case of the remote control, it switches the set on and off, changes the channels and adjusts the volume.

Benefits explain what the advantages will do for the customer. They answer the question, 'What does it [feature] do [advantage] for the customer [benefit]?'. In the case of the remote control (feature) it switches the set on and off, changes the channels and adjusts the volume (advantages) while you relax in your chair (benefit). Benefits appeal to the customer's 'motives to buy'. Principal buying motives include enjoyment, pride, security, prestige, wealth, usefulness, savings and value. In the remote control example, the motives to buy were 'enjoyment and usefulness'.

Handling objections

Once you have made the presentation you can expect the customer to raise objections. Objections at this stage take the form of the customer simply requesting more information or asking for clarification. There are a few common objections and ways to handle or answer them. Here are three types of objections frequently raised in traditional sales programmes.

A request for information

The customer may require more information about your product or service. Normally you are advised to give an accurate answer and include FAB.

Example

Customer: 'What is the Bosch Jetronic fuel injection system?'

Salesperson: 'It's a system for accurately metering the fuel into the engine, as required by the current driving conditions. So it saves you fuel and money while giving optimum performance.'

Price objection

This is the type of objection most feared by the salesperson. The advice here is to ascertain with what the customer is comparing your product or service, then overcome the objection by selling your benefits.

Example

Customer: 'I have seen a comparable model and it's much cheaper.'
Salesperson: 'When you say "a comparable model", do you remember exactly what the model number and size was?'
Customer: 'Not really.'
Salesperson: 'Well, let me explain, there are several models that look alike but are very different when it comes to performance. This one has... .'

Excuses to delay a decision

The customer might say, 'I want to think about it' or 'I want to discuss it with my spouse/partner'. Here, the customer is not totally convinced, and this is not a true objection. You now have to uncover the true objection by asking, 'When you say you aren't sure about this, is it because of something I haven't mentioned yet?'

Objections can all be overcome if you continue the conversation, unearth the true objection and give the appropriate benefits.

Closing techniques

You are now at the final stage of the sale – asking for the order. There are numerous ways in which this can be done. Here are the most common.

The direct question close

Here you ask a direct question and wait for the customer to answer.

Example

Salesperson: 'Will you be taking delivery today?'

The alternative close

This is one of the most common and popular closes; you simply give the customer a choice.

Example

Salesperson: 'Would you like us to finance it or are you going to pay cash?'

The minor point close

Of course, the major point is 'Are you going to buy it?'. By taking the customer's mind away from the major point and focusing on a minor point you can often close the sale.

Example

Salesperson: 'Which colour do you prefer?'

The special opportunity close

This could be a sale – a well known retailing ploy – a clearance, or closing down sale. This is a common closing technique that is based on the assumption that everyone loves a bargain.

Example

Salesperson: 'This model goes back to its normal price on Monday. I suggest you buy it now.'

The second opinion close

When all else fails, in order not to lose the sale, you may wish to call a salesperson or manager for assistance. Known in the trade as the TO (turnover), you simply introduce another salesperson and explain how far the sale has progressed.

Example

Salesperson: 'Let me introduce my manager, Mr Roberts. Mr Roberts, our customer, Miss Jameson, is interested in this office plan. I told her you were an expert in layout so I wonder if you could help. This it what she needs... .'

There are many other closing techniques, but the above examples should give you a good idea of how they work. At the close, you should also take some type of action to show the customer that you have closed the sale, like writing up the order or shaking hands.

Once you have closed you might consider selling add-ons or a second item, since the customer is now in a buying mood and is more likely to be receptive.

Review

Consider these sales basics in the light of the material you have covered in Part One. Where do they fit into the Sales Mind Matrix? How do they meet the requirements of the truth-seeking brain? What are their strengths and weaknesses?

PART TWO

Information: the new wealth

Introduction

In Part One, you discovered how to use your Sales Mind Matrix, your salesenses together with your magnificent sales memory. Part Two starts your sale in the right direction. You will find out how to accelerate your learning to gain knowledge about your products, services, ideas and then about yourself!

First, you will learn how to become an instant information expert. We live in an information economy: information has become the new wealth. Each day, more and more information becomes available on any subject you may care to mention. You have to decide on your area of expertise and then keep up with the daily knowledge explosion of your choice. You will discover, in Part Two, how to become an information expert in a matter of days!

The knowledge explosion is not confined to what we sell but also to the seller, the salesperson him or herself. We now have a wealth of information about the mind–body connection and how important this is to superior sales performance. In today's hectic and stressful society, knowing how to take care of yourself is a critical component to a successful sales career. We cover this subject with a series of Skill Builders that are fun and easy to do.

Chapter 4, 'Infocentre: Be a Sales Authority', gives you the keys to mastering information in this 'information age'. Once you have realized that you are constantly selling information, you have made the shift into the information age. You must think of yourself as 'an information centre', able to answer any questions on your product or service. You need to be an 'Infocentre' to satisfy your customers' continuous demands for information.

Chapter 5, 'Mind Maps®: The Fast Track to Infocentre Fame', deals with a new whole-brain technique known as Mind Mapping. This breakthrough in Sales Mind Matrix learning enables you to absorb rapidly, and retain, large amounts of information with instant recall! Once you are an 'Infocentre expert' you will find selling easier and more enjoyable. Your new knowledge will give you a new confidence and growing sales success.

Chapter 6 is called 'Insight. The Mind–Body Connection'. Understanding the mind–body connection gives insights into how these two parts must work in harmony for superior sales performance. This chapter gives formulas on how to get both your mind and body into shape. Through a series of Skill Builders, and armed with new information, you will soon be in the top 10 per cent of 'Olympic' salespeople and enjoying your new sales status.

The chapters that follow will show how you can:

- communicate better;
- apply your brain power to selling power;
- become an expert in product/service information;
- have customers calling you for advice and to give you orders;
- motivate yourself for higher performance;
- enjoy effective, fun-filled workdays;
- have unlimited **satisfied customers**.

As we mentioned in Part One, to make the best use of these materials first skim rapidly through the chapters to get a general understanding. Then read them in depth and do all the Skill Builders in the proper sequence. For maximum benefit we recommend that you spend a week on each chapter, giving yourself time for in-depth reading, study, practice-time for the Skill Builders and time for your brain to absorb and integrate all the new material into your everyday sales behaviours.

Once again, to speed up the mastery of these new materials we strongly recommend that you talk about them to your family, friends and peers at work. If you belong to a club, association or group, make a short presentation on any aspect of the book you wish.

When you have finished the in-depth reading, keep *Brain Sell* with you for daily reference. You will be surprised at the new thoughts, new ideas and new techniques you will develop. Keep a record of these new thoughts and ideas.

Finally, keep practising the Skill Builders that make up Part Two. Reading the material alone will not allow a transfer of these skills into your everyday behavioural repertoire. Continuous practice will.

4   Infocentre

Be a sales authority

You know the answer

Imagine going to work tomorrow and noticing something different. It has nothing to do with your appearance, your mannerisms, or behaviours, but it has everything to do with your mind. You find, much to your delight, that your mind has become a power house of *information*. As you think of a subject – any subject – a stream of knowledge flows into your mind. It's as though you have some secret way to tap into all the libraries of the world and instantly extract all the connected knowledge you need on that subject!

You wonder if this new phenomenal ability will last. Imagine your excitement when it does! At work, you can answer correctly any questions. Every time a customer calls on the phone for information, you give the answers because *you* are the expert!

You have become an information centre, or 'infocentre'. Now you are an expert on your company's products and services, what do you think will happen to your sales? Or to your position within the company? Your job satisfaction? This chapter will show you how you can rapidly become an *infocentre*.

Overview

In our modern business world, there is one thing more important than money – knowledge. Today's knowledge creates tomorrow's wealth. By becoming an information expert on any subject of your choice you will have a bright sales future! Modern customers want added value in the form of information. Having that information instantly available on the products, services and ideas that you sell ensures that you have made the shift into the 'information age', and the rewards will follow.

Infoswap

Christine Martindale started her own company in 1980 with $15 000 cash and one telephone, selling imported cut flowers to florists throughout the USA. The wholesale cut-flower business is brutally competitive, with customers hopping from company to company in search of the lowest price. But Christine decided to take a different approach to sales. By helping her florists to build their own businesses, she would also build a loyal group of customers for her company, Esprit Miami.

To build her customer base, Christine sought the help of IM International, a fashion forecast company that predicts designer colours two years ahead. Next she travelled to Italy and Colombia to persuade her growers to plant flowers in the predicted 'fashionable' colours. Two years later when these flowers arrived in the USA, Christine repacked them to ensure that her retail florists received them in mint condition.

'Designer-coloured flowers' were a hit. Dona Christie, as her Colombian suppliers named her, never looked back. When Richard designed a selling skills programme for her telephone salespeople in 1985, she was handling more than 300 accounts, and sales had climbed past $7 million. While her competitors are still battling it out over price, Christine has created her own special niche in the marketplace.

When asked to account for her success, Christine said, 'I realized that I was in a competitive business. If I could get some small advantage just to give me an edge, then I would have a chance. The *information* provided by IM International did just that!'

Become the expert

In today's high-tech information society, the salespeople who become experts on their products or services will succeed in the marketplace. Customers want facts and information. They want to be sure they're making the right decision. They have to rely on your knowledge.

In his best seller, *POWERSHIFT*, Alvin Toffler spells out how important knowledge will be for the rest of our working lives as we enter the 'knowledge economy'. Toffler predicts '...when knowledge resources are recognized as the most important of all, employee remuneration may well come to hinge, at least in part, on the success of each person in adding value to the corporate knowledge reserve. In turn, we can expect even more sophisticated power struggles for the control of knowledge assets and the process that generates them.'

President Clinton continually tells the American people, 'It is clear that what you earn will depend upon what you learn.' He stresses the importance of lifelong learning and being well educated in order to compete in the new global economy.

You and your customers are playing infoswap – the customer needs your expert information and you need him or her to be totally satisfied. In order to do this, you must first ascertain a clear picture of his or her information needs and then be able to meet them. Infoswap is your ability to swap information, resulting in a satisfied customer.

As products and services become increasingly complex, selling in the future will depend more than ever on your expertise. The customer's demand for information and facts will only continue to grow.

First you must decide on your area of sales expertise! Give this some thought, as it's an important decision. For which product/s and or service/s do you want to be known as the expert?

Skill Builder 22: the expert

Complete the sentence in the box below.

My area of expertise is

Skill Builder 23: present knowledge level

How much do you know about the products or services that you're currently selling? Answer the 'Yes/No' questions in the self-scoring test below to gain some insight into your present level of infoswap.

	YES	NO

1. Do you read at least one trade journal each week?
2. Do your peers ask you for information?
3. Have you presented information at a sales meeting in the last month?
4. Does your management ask for your opinion on what is selling?
5. Do you know your policy on returns without having to refer to it?
6. Can you name ten customers and their last purchase?
7. Do you know the names of your three main competitors?
8. Do you read the instructions on the items you are selling?
9. Have you recently received letters from customers, thanking you for your help?
10. Can you name the item you sold the most of last month, including the top ten sellers and the percentages of each item?

TOTAL SCORE

If you scored more than eight 'yeses' you are an authority on your products/service category, and this chapter will help you to manage that knowledge more effectively. If you scored less than eight, help is on its way!

A fast way to increase sales

In the late 1980s, when Richard was commissioned to design a service and selling skills programme for a regional mall in the south-eastern USA, 86 of the 104 traders requested 'increased product knowledge of their salespeople' as their top priority and the fastest way they knew to increase sales! Their request came as no surprise: better product and service knowledge has been the number one request from our clients worldwide.

Customers' biggest complaint

Lack of knowledge angers the customer. According to a recent survey published in *The Wall Street Journal*, poorly informed salespeople are one of customers' biggest complaints.

In January 1994, *The Miami Herald* reported a study by the prestigious research firm, Yankelovich and Partners. The researchers had conducted random telephone interviews throughout the USA during October and November, 1993 – '60 per cent of all respondents claimed they had asked a question which a salesperson couldn't answer'.

Whilst you might agree that becoming an expert would improve your sales, in the back of your mind, you're probably thinking, 'Does that mean I'll have to spend all my free time memorizing facts and reading service manuals? It's a good idea, but that's too much like homework, and I had more than enough of that in school!' Well, we have good news for you! Recent research on how your brain works will make learning and remembering your product or service information a breeze. You can now rapidly become an expert and succeed at infoswap; start by completing Skill Builder 24 on page 82.

As we mentioned in Part One, Chapter 1, 'Whole-Brain Selling', the left cortical skills are dominantly analytical, responsible for logic, words, numbers, details and lists. Since most of your time at school was spent developing these left cortical skills, your product/service fact sheet probably looks something like the example in Figure 4.1 on page 83.

Skill Builder 24: a fact sheet

Here's a Skill Builder to start you thinking. Select a product or service that you are selling. Take five minutes to write up a fact sheet in the space below, including all the information you know about it. Please do this before proceeding to page 83.

Selected item: _____ (product/service)

Facts about this item:

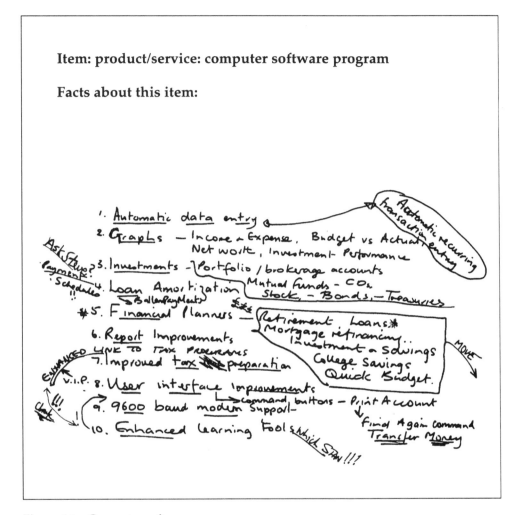

Figure 4.1   Computer software

Did your product/service fact sheet look anything like that in the Figure? Was it in a linear format, written from left to right, top to bottom of the page, in list format? This is the way you learned to write and take notes. But, nowadays, this linear method is less than 50 per cent efficient.

First, writing down facts this way is slow work. Did you find your thoughts going faster than you could write? Did you find yourself going back over what you had written and checking your spelling and grammar? Did you have to write down extra words to link the main ideas together? Second, it's dull to write this way – and it's boring to read. You're always tempted to stop writing before you've finished thinking. Third, taking notes this way requires only logical thought. You have to plan your thoughts correctly and write down the facts in sequence. What happens if you miss something? Do you start all over again, use the eraser, or squeeze it in somewhere?

FAB

How have we been learning product information up to now? The main thrust since the 1940s has been 'Benefit Selling' (see the Appendix to Part One for a more detailed explanation).

Benefit Selling takes product knowledge and breaks it into a three-part format:

1.   Features
2.   Advantages
3.   Benefits

or FAB, for short. All products and services can be broken down into a number of features which in turn have both respective advantages and benefits. The FAB formula is then used to answer a customer's expressed needs. 'Benefit Selling' has been used extensively over the last 50 years and is still widely taught today.

Its disadvantages

When Richard conducted sales training programmes around the world – from Massey Ferguson in the USA, to Van Der Meer in the Netherlands, to Honda in South Africa, to Reader's Digest in the UK, to Arnotts in Ireland, to Meyer Emporium in Australia, to Hertie in Germany – sales managers always insisted that he train their staff in FAB. Why? Because customers complained constantly about lack of product information, and the sales managers saw FAB as the answer.

FAB sheets were duly written for the clients' products and services and introduced to the salespeople. Initially they were excited about FAB, but within a few months it was difficult to find a FAB sheet in sight! The early enthusiasm was soon lost. After analysing more than 1000 sales conversations, we realized why the FAB concept for 50 years has had disappointing results in selling.

First, within 24 hours of the training, the participants forgot more than 80 per cent of what they had learned (this is standard memory loss over a 24-hour period), and very few salespeople reviewed their product information (FAB sheets) after the initial training.

Second, the salespeople often failed to use the FAB concept correctly. Instead of giving the customer the appropriate benefit statement in response to his or her question, or expressed need, they inundated the customer with all or some of the product features in a 'hit or miss' approach. This cost both time and sales.

Currently, millions of pounds and thousands of hours are wasted daily on sales training programmes without the salespeople getting the full pay-off. You don't have to suffer the same fate. In the next section, we'll show you how to spend one to two minutes a day reviewing new materials, and you will soon have that knowledge safely stored in your long-term memory.

The added value formula

In our service economy, customers are demanding better service and better value. This translates into an insatiable demand for quality information. Customers want information. They want to know everything from the names of satisfied clients to the construction materials, to the competitors' products. They want to know the prices and the new developments in the industry. They read the latest advertisements, trade journals and consumer magazines. They want to learn everything about your products and services! EVERYTHING.

Consider, for a moment, your role in the economic cycle of selling. A manufacturer has produced a product or range of products that you are selling, or you offer some type of service: maybe financial, security or home decorating. What you bring to that product or service is the added value for which the customer is willing to pay a premium price. That added value, in most instances, is information – quality information. The current unprecedented availability of information on every topic under the sun gives you a unique opportunity.

You have decided on your area of expertise (see Skill Builder 22, page 79) whether it be shoelaces, jet planes, retirement plans or mobile phones. Next, you must become an expert on the subject so that you will be able to add value for your customer – value in the form of the most recent, accurate information on the subject of your choice. Decide on your information sources and immediately start to collect all the information you can. In Chapter 5 we will explain how to store this vast amount of information in your long-term memory, with ease.

Almost daily, new businesses are started by people who study information and look for new ways to market this information in *the last four feet*. Take the case of Antony van Graan. When Antony returned to Johannesburg from a vacation in Holland he discovered that he had missed the North Sea Jazz Festival because he was not aware it was held during the month he was there. He wondered how many other people had had similar disappointing experiences because of their lack of knowledge about what was happening in a country they were about to visit? He phoned several travel agents only to find that they too did not know what was on. So he invested in a computer and launched 'The Traveller's Diary', a detailed, regularly updated listing, covering important concerts, events, trade fairs and exhibitions in western Europe. He soon had the listings available by subscription to travel agents throughout his native South Africa.

Antony's story is but one of many. He first decided on his area of expertise, then he collected information from different sources, added value by listing it in an attractive format, 'The Traveller's Diary', then sold it by subscription on the South African Airways computer – *the last four feet*. He simply swapped information for money – a true 'infoswap'.

If you know everything about your product or service, you will find a way to use that information in your sales presentation. The result of your infoswap will be higher sales for you and a knowledgeable, satisfied customer who is likely to return and buy something from you again in the future.

This chapter outlines the critical role which information will play in your career, in this 'information age'. You have to become an infocentre, constantly exchanging information with your customer.

You need in-depth, up-to-date, expert information on your products and services to succeed in selling. Up to now, FAB (Features, Advantages and Benefits) product information sheets have formed the main thrust of learning product information. However, your customers want more – they want up-to-date quality information. They want to know everything there is to know about what they are buying. Being able to supply this information is the added value that will result in a satisfied customer who will buy from you and return again and again.

Review

Today, whatever products or services you sell, you need to know far more than its features, advantages and benefits. You need quality information which gives you that added value to your product or service. You need a far broader knowledge of everything you are selling, your competitors and market trends. After all, this is 'the information age'.

You can get up-to-date, quality information from reading trade magazines, speaking to satisfied users, talking to competitors, watching television, reading the newspaper or tapping other sources. It is a continuous learning process that makes you an expert and an infocentre. But, how can you 'fast-learn' quality information? How can you develop the ability to recall information at will and become an expert infocentre? The answer, to be found in Chapter 6, will surprise and delight you in its ease and simplicity.

Skill Builder 25: infocentre review

On a separate piece of blank paper, summarize this chapter, 'Infocentre'. You may look back.

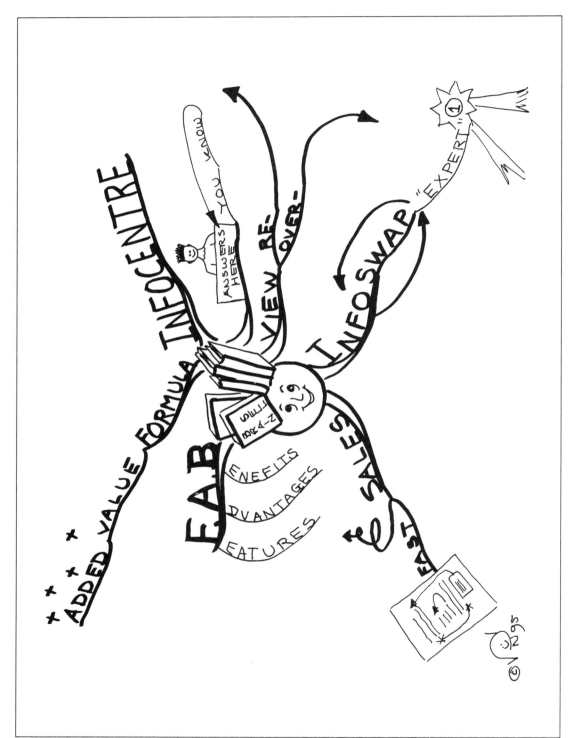

Figure 4.2 Mind Map: infocentre

5 Mind Maps®

The fast track to infocentre fame

A revolution in learning

Imagine you are a child again, attending school. A new teacher, Ms Brainchild, has been appointed to your class. On the first day of school Ms Brainchild arrives. She is a beautiful woman whose bright, twinkling blue eyes and wonderful smile radiate energy and love, and she shows that she cares by the way she listens and answers questions. You feel the excitement in the air as she asks the class the following questions:

'Who would like to spend less time studying and more time playing?'

Everyone raises their hands.

'Who would like to remember everything they were taught in class, without ever again having to revise for exams?'

All the children's hands go up.

Then Ms Brainchild announces that she has a new, wonderful learning technique that is so easy that you can learn it in five minutes, so powerful that you will find schoolwork becomes fun work, so interesting that you will never again be bored in class and so wonderful that your brain will thank you for learning it.

If you missed it at school, you have another chance, for here in this chapter of *Brain Sell* is this new technique that is revolutionizing learning around the globe, and can do the same for you!

Overview

Mind Mapping is a new learning technology which allows you to use your Sales Mind Matrix in an accelerated learning process. It enables you to retain large volumes of information easily and to recall it in fractions of a second, making you an expert on the subjects of your choice. This chapter shows you how to develop this skill.

Mind Maps®

Tony developed a technology he named Mind Maps® which allows the complete Sales Mind Matrix to work in harmony, resulting in a better way to record, remember and use information. In his new bestseller *The Mind Map Book* (BBC Publications, 1993), Tony gives a detailed account of the history, development and applications of Mind Maps.

A Mind Map is a simple thinking tool which enables you to capture all the information you need to know about your product or service, on just *one* piece of paper. And, unlike traditional memorizing of facts, Mind Mapping is fun to do!

The following pages show you how to develop a Mind Map and how to apply it to your products or services. This is followed by a technique that requires only a few minutes of your day to absorb vast amounts of new information and, finally, suggestions for numerous business applications of Mind Maps. We decided to use a salesperson as our working example to illustrate how any subject can be Mind Mapped!

Step 1: an image is worth 1000 words

Follow this format on your own separate sheet. Start by drawing a picture of your product or service in the very centre of your page. Images or pictures make a powerful impact on the brain and are easier to remember than words. Draw that image as the central theme of your Mind Map to start the creative process. Don't worry about your drawing skills, your central image will always be understood by you. Use three colours or more for your central image, give it dimension, and do not put it in a frame or bubble.

Figure 5.1 Central image

Step 2: tree of thought

Just as we have branches on a tree, so we have shaped branches on our Mind Map to represent the essential ideas or topics (see Figure 5.2). All the branches start from the central image. Branches reflect nature, being thick near the base and organic and curved to attract the eye. They should be connected to the centre, as the brain remembers better that which is connected. Each branch should hold a key idea or topic condensed into one word or image. Use one word/image per line throughout your Mind Map, printing your words as upright as possible to make them easier to read and remember. In this context, these branches could include price, advantages, construction, materials and instructions of use or assembly.

Figure 5.2 Branches

Step 3: link words and ideas

Draw smaller branches off your main topics, as new thoughts and ideas come to mind (see Figure 5.3). You can add them using words, pictures, colours, symbols or codes. As in the Sales Mind Matrix, you will be incorporating all, or as many of, the ten mental skills as possible. Then link words and ideas, showing clearly how one idea relates to another. You can clean up your Mind Map later if it becomes cluttered or untidy.

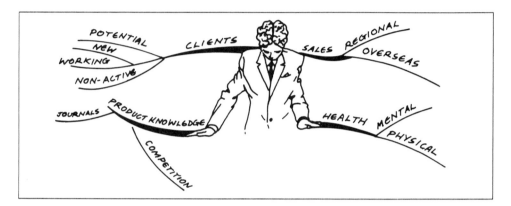

Figure 5.3 Links

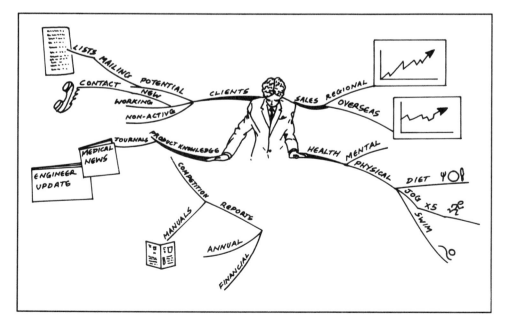

Figure 5.4 Codes

Step 4: codes, colours and pictures

Use colours, pictures and codes to highlight different points and to show relationships between the different branches of your map (see Figure 5.4). Use pictures and images wherever possible to stimulate your creativity and improve your memory – for example: brand photos; symbols, codes of departments; and colours. Incorporate as many of the mental skills appearing in the Sales Mind Matrix as possible.

Step 5: consolidate key concepts and ideas

Develop your Mind Map as fast as you can and for as long as possible. If you find yourself slowing down, add blank lines to encourage extra thoughts or go to another branch – push yourself to try to speed up and record everything you can. When you have exhausted all your ideas, go back over your Mind Map to organize and consolidate your thoughts into patterns that make sense to you. Do this by using highlighter colours, numbers, arrows, variations in size of printing, line and image, spacing, codes or outlining the branches as shown in Figure 5.5. Use arrows to make connections within and across the branch pattern. The completed Mind

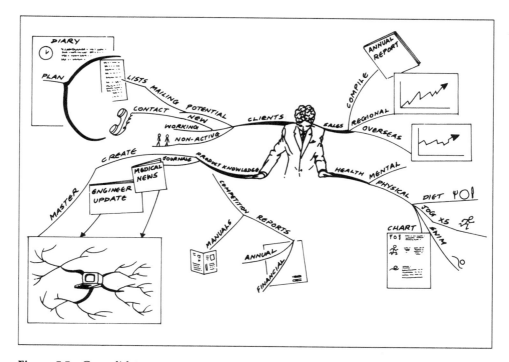

Figure 5.5 Consolidate

Map will reflect your personal style and make sense to you. It will be an application of your Sales Mind Matrix, from that first central image to the whole picture, all on one piece of paper!

Summary of the Mind Map laws

1. **Use emphasis.**

    *   Always use a central image.
    *   Use images throughout your Mind Map.
    *   Use three or more colours per central image.
    *   Use dimension in images.
    *   Use synaesthesia (blending of senses).
    *   Use variations in size of printing, line and image.
    *   Use organized spacing.

2. **Use association.**

    *   Use arrows when you want to make connections within or across the branch pattern.
    *   Use colours.
    *   Use codes.

3. **Be clear.**

    *   Use only one key word per line.
    *   Print all words.
    *   Print key words on lines.
    *   Make line length equal to word length.
    *   Connect lines to other lines.
    *   Make the central lines thicker and organically curved (like tree branches).
    *   Make your boundaries 'embrace' your branch outline.
    *   Make your images as clear as possible.
    *   Keep your printing as upright as possible.

Mind Map Master

Why do Mind Maps work so well in organizing product and service information? They harness all the power of your brain, making it easy to remember the important ideas. The colours, images and key words are much easier for your brain to recall than long, complicated sentences because they reduce the quantity of words by up to 90 per cent. Most importantly, Mind Maps are another way of illustrating the Sales Mind Matrix!

Mind Mapping can help everyone – executives, managers, salespeople, consultants, university and high school students and home makers – to improve rapidly their skill to take in and remember information. Mind Maps enable you to master quality information and become an infocentre expert within days!

Mind Maps are easy to design and easy to incorporate into your sales presentations. In less than 10 minutes, you can draw a Mind Map for one of your major product categories, review it and immediately put your knowledge to work. All you need are some coloured marker pens and white paper.

Like any new skill, learning how to Mind Map needs practice. If you are serious about becoming a high sales achiever and mastering *the last four feet*, we encourage you to take advantage of this new exciting breakthrough in learning. As with any skill, the more you practise Mind Mapping, the faster and more proficient you will become. The formula below will make you an expert in your chosen speciality in a few short weeks.

Get the facts

Gather up all the popular magazines, newsletters and trade journals you can find in your area of interest. There are hundreds of trade journals published constantly that cover almost every type of product or service. If you don't subscribe to many publications, visit your local library, taking along your marker pens and a large piece of paper to capture the information on a Mind Map.

Rapidly scan the entire collection of gathered information in a few minutes to get an overview of the contents.

Look for items of interest

Next, draw a picture of the topic of interest in the centre of your Mind Map. Go through one of the publications again, this time reading the items appertaining to your central image, and capture these ideas as separate branches. Remember, you can put everything from these journals on the one page, by applying the rules of Mind Mapping covered in this chapter.

Sometimes you may wish to have a separate, in-depth Mind Map of important subjects for future reference and study.

Connect items

You will notice that some items in the journal are connected to each other. Maybe an article on computers on page 6 is linked to another computer article on page 12. One branch of your Mind Map might be 'computers' with sub-branches on each of these two stories. That's why the first scan of the journal is so important in helping you pick out the items of interest.

When you have finished the journal, review and scan it again to make sure you have captured everything you want!

Review

Take your one-page Mind Map and place it somewhere at home or at work where you can see and review it. If you think of more ideas at any time, add them to your Mind Map. Remember that 80 per cent of what you read is forgotten in 24 hours unless you review the material daily. Most salespeople will forget everything they've read in a few days. You will stay an expert if you review your Mind Maps daily for a minimum of 7 days.

Consolidate

The following month, go to the library again and put together another Mind Map on the next trade journal. Then repeat the process for a third month. After three months, consolidate your three Mind Maps onto one new Master Mind Map. Soon, you'll have more knowledge of your products than the rest of the sales force combined!

Build a knowledge base

Once you have developed a series of Mind Maps and reviewed them, you will be well on the way to building your knowledge base, ensuring that you are an expert on the subject of your choice.

Skill Builder 26: build a knowledge base

On a separate sheet of blank paper, Mind Map the products or services you sell, and the facts that you need to know to become an expert. Add to this any of your company rules: for example, 'policies on returns', or 'conditions of employment'. Include the names and items sold by five main competitors. Have a branch 'industry trends' where you can record what is happening in your industry. Have a branch 'company news' to keep track of all the news and developments within your organization.

Study the example in Figure 5.6. We took the subject of 'Management', selected six popular bestselling books and Mind Mapped them (on a single page). The books were: *Megatrends 2000: Ten New Directions for the 1990s* by John Naisbitt and Patricia Aburdene (William Morrow); *What They Don't Teach You at Harvard Business School: Notes from a Street-Smart Executive* by Mark H. McCormack (Bantam Books); *The Managerial Mystique: Restoring Leadership in Business* by Abraham Zaleznick (Harper & Row); *A Passion for Excellence* by Tom Peters and Nancy Austin (Random House); *The Greatest Management Principle in the World* by Michael LeBoeuf (Berkley-Books); *Managing Conflict*, The Great American Bathroom Book (Compact Classic).

From your previous Mind Map created in Skill Builder 26, start building individual Mind Maps on specific topics which you want to enlarge on.

1. Get a pad of blank (non-lined) white paper and some coloured marker pens.
2. Include, on each Mind Map, everything you know about the specific topics you have selected.
3. Notice that the Mind Map is dynamic. Like the 'Tree of Thought', branches will grow with new ideas.
4. Continually update and review these Mind Maps.

Know even more

Soon you will have a specific Mind Map for each of the subjects you originally Mind Mapped. Review them, add to them, and develop new ones. Notice that the more you know, *the easier it is to know even more!*

Here is another great secret in *Brain Sell*. Once your brain has certain knowledge, it finds it easier to add additional knowledge to the existing knowledge base. So becoming an expert becomes *easier and easier.*

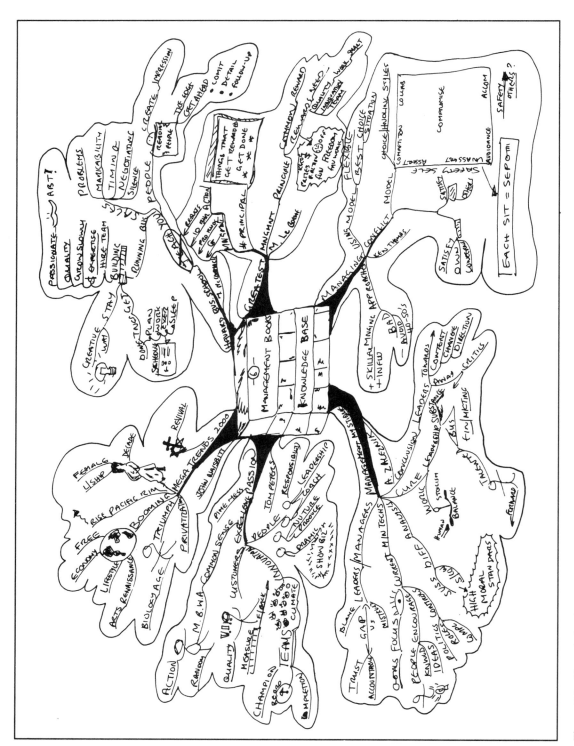

Figure 5.6 Knowledge base

Remember me

What makes a customer return to the same salesperson? While acting as a consultant to K.G. Men's Stores in Denver, Richard ran a series of focus groups (a panel of consumers who answer questions about their buying habits). When asked the question 'What makes you return?', the group members replied, 'Salespeople who remember me, remember my previous purchases and remember what clothing styles suit me.'

Many unsuccessful salespeople believe that they have poor memories. As you now know, that's not true. Your brain has the potential to remember more than all the books stored in the libraries in the world. So, remembering a few hundred of your best customer's names, recent purchases and buying preferences is well within your mental reach.

Customer profiles

Through Mind Maps, you can capture and recall important information and link important sales ideas together. You can use these techniques to build simple customer sales Mind Maps that will improve your customer contact.

Here's an example. Jean Baker, a salesperson for a Hampstead estate agent is talking to a Mrs Wardel. Mrs Wardel apparently wants to buy a freehold flat for her and her sister. They want two bedrooms, one bathroom, a kitchen and a large living/dining room, ideally with a small garden and preferably near the Underground as they have no car and cannot walk far due to poor health. Mrs Wardel owns a printing company, Rapid Press, in Leyton and her sister is the accountant. They are willing to pay up to £150,000 and would like to find something suitable by next January. Jean has nothing that matches Mrs Wardel's ideal flat at present but says she will start to look. When Mrs Wardel has left Jean takes out a small pad and, in a few minutes, draws a Mind Map on Mrs Wardel desired flat.

Next, Jean must find a way to link this Mind Map with Mrs Wardel in order to help her remember her customer's name and information the next time she contacts her. Because Mrs Wardel walks with a slight waddle and her name, Wardel, is close to waddle, Jean draws a duck on her Mind Map and adds the words 'waddle'. Now, test your own powers of memory.

Figure 5.7   Mrs Wardel

Skill Builder 27: Mrs Wardel

> Close the book and draw Jean's customer file on Mrs Wardel, without
> looking back.

Easier and faster

When they try this customer profile Mind Mapping technique on their best
customers, many salespeople are astonished at the details they recall.
Remembering the important information becomes easier and faster each
time you practise. Your memory is like a muscle; it needs Skill Builders to
keep in shape, and the stronger your memory gets, the better it does, with
less effort.

As you have discovered, it takes less than a few minutes to complete a customer profile Mind Map. It would take you less than 10 minutes a day to scan your top *50* customers' Mind Maps profiles. Just think what remembering all that information would do to your sales!

The power of sales Mind Maps

Imagine the follow-up sales conversation, when Jean contacts Mrs Wardel by phone:

Jean: 'Good morning, Mrs Wardel. Jean Baker, your estate agent. How's Rapid Press doing?'

Mrs Wardel: 'We are having a good month, Jean. Any news on my flat?'

Jean: 'Did you get the listings I sent you in the post?'

Mrs Wardel: 'Yes, my sister and I looked at them last night.'

Jean: 'Did you notice the flat in Eldon Grove that I highlighted?'

Mrs Wardel: 'Yes, we saw it.'

Jean: 'I thought it ideal for you both as it's a quarter of a mile from Hampstead Underground station, and you said that it was important for you both to live within walking distance of the Tube.'

Mrs Wardel: 'Yes, it did seem perfect at first, but we don't want to walk up the hill to get to the Tube station each morning.'

Jean: 'Mrs Wardel, you don't have to. When you come home you get off at Hampstead, so you walk down the hill. When you go to work you walk down the hill and get on at Belsize Park.'

Mrs Wardel: (after a pause) 'What a wonderful idea!'

Jean: 'Can I make an appointment for you to see it tonight?'

Mrs Wardel: 'Yes, by all means. We could be at your office by five.'

Jean: 'Look forward to seeing you both at five, then, Mrs Wardel.'

After Jean has finished the conversation, she makes the appointment for 5 p.m. with the flat owners and updates her Mind Map.

That's how easy it is to use Mind Maps to develop successful customer profiles as a sales tool.

Skill Builder 28: build a customer base

Now, since your brain can store millions of these customer files, why not start with ten of your best customers? Once you have ten you can build a larger base. Have a special pad for your customer Sales Mind Maps. Make certain the pages are unlined and have coloured pens handy.

On each customer Sales Mind Map, put down as much information as you know (you'll be surprised at how much you do remember) or, if you already have customer files, convert these to sales Mind Maps. Start now and update them as your customers make purchases and you gather more information on them.

Can you imagine what will happen to your sales performance and income as you build a strong customer base. The sales Mind Map is the ideal tool to help you do just that, and it's *easy*!

Mind Map a customer base

To review, here are the 11 steps to create customer sales Mind Maps:

1. Develop a strong image of the customer in the centre of your page.
2. Branch off your central image with the essential topics – for example, preferences, purchases, personal details, future purchases.
3. Rapidly complete the sales Mind Map with all the information you have available.
4. Link all key words and ideas using colours, pictures, codes and symbols.
5. Consolidate key concepts and ideas.
6. Store your sales Mind Maps in strong, easily accessible ring binders.
7. Have a daily review schedule, where you spend time going through your customer sales Mind Maps. One glance will remind you of all the important issues and small details you need to know.
8. During the review, update your customer sales Mind Maps with all recent developments – for example, new product arrivals.
9. Colour-code actions to be taken – for example use a certain colour to indicate that you should contact certain customers with information of newly arrived products and then follow up.
10. Update each customer's sales Mind Map whenever he or she makes a purchase or you gather any information.
11. Make your customer's sales Mind Maps a working tool in your daily sales routine. Refer to them, update them, sell from them and enjoy them!

Business MMapplications (Mind Map Applications)

Corporations and individuals worldwide have devised many business 'MMapplications'. Here are a few.

Acer Computers

Max Hung, President of Acer Computers, Miami, uses Mind Maps to increase his sales force's knowledge of both his own line of computers and those of his competitors. Max also uses Mind Maps for his personal goals. Luis Vecchi, the Sales Director at Acer, uses a Mind Map for each of his South American distributors. They display Acer sales, its targets and market share, as well as its major competitors.

Interpolis

Jan Pieter H. Six, Vice President of Interpolis, a Dutch insurance company, used a Mind Map to structure an entire organization. He also uses it to act as a stabilizing vision for the company, with great success.

Association International Management

Thomas H. Schaper of the Association International Management in Germany, uses Mind Maps for time and self-management. His Mind Maps have made him an expert on these topics.

Hewlett Packard

Jean-Luc Kastner of Hewlett Packard Medical Products Group, Europe, designed a 'Cardiac Arrhythmia' Training Course for their support engineers, using Mind Maps. First, the course was designed as Mind Map flipcharts. From the Mind Map flipchart presentations trainees developed their own Master Mind Maps which were posted on the walls of the training room. As the course progressed, students tested their knowledge against a computer-aided training tool that simulated patients' electrocardiograms (ECGs). At the end of each day the students copied the Master Mind Maps into their own Mind Map pads for review. The course proved to be a remarkable success in that students remembered a greater percentage of the material, both in the short and long term.

Temple Marketing

Nigel Temple, President of Temple Marketing in Britain, uses Mind Maps to plan the marketing needs of every customer. They consist of: the range of products the client wishes to market; the client's business and marketing objectives; the prime messages the client wishes to convey to the public and the medium by which they wish to do so; the nature and structure of the consultancy agreements; the use of various media and their inclusion or exclusion in the overall marketing response; and the target markets in the near, mid- and long-term future.

CuCo's Mexican Restaurantes

Vincent Liuzza Jr, President of CuCo's Mexican Restaurantes, in Louisiana, uses Mind Maps to improve customer service and strategic planning. By designing a Master Mind Map which is available to everyone – including management and the dish washer – he achieves an open corporate culture and generates winning ideas. One such idea was from a waiter who suggested, on the Mind Map branch related to security problems in the restaurant's car park, 'Why not walk the customers to their cars?' The idea was used, and the customer count at the restaurants soared.

Fidelity Investments®

Bruce Johnstone, a mutual fund Senior Executive with Fidelity Investments of Boston, has used Mind Maps throughout his career. He Mind Maps the interview with companies in which he is considering investing Fidelity's money, and claims that he has made successful investments due to the summary abilities of Mind Maps.

University of The West Indies

Keith Mansion, Director of Information Systems Strategic Planning at The University of The West Indies, Kingston, Jamaica, uses Mind Maps to plan his complex computer network.

Institute of Chartered Accountants

Award-winning students in the English Institute of Chartered Accountants use Mind Maps to prepare for their examinations as do tax advisers in such prestigious companies as Price Waterhouse for problem solving and advising clients on financial matters.

EDS

Electronic Data Systems (EDS), the global information systems conglomerate, uses Mind Maps to teach Mental Literacy, in-house (General Motors) and to become a learning organization.

Boeing Aircraft

Dr Stanley condensed an engineering manual into a 25-foot Mind Map, reducing the time taken to learn the information from years to just a few weeks. Boeing estimated the training cost savings at $11 million.

These are just a few of the MMapplications in existence. On reading this wide range of MMapplications, you might have had a few ideas on how you can use Mind Maps in your organization or in your sales! The following Skill Builder enables you to capture these ideas.

Skill Builder 29: MMapplications

On a separate sheet, construct a Mind Map of how you could use Mind Maps in your organization.

Review

Today's customers want added value in the form of quality information. By improving your knowledge, you can become an expert, an infocentre and a quality information provider (QIP). QIPs are salespeople who use their Sales Mind Matrix to its full potential.

A fast and effective method to remember important information is to Mind Map it. This new tool allows you to take in massive amounts of information, store it and recall it at will. Mind Maps help in recalling information, organizing thinking, focusing on the whole picture, and in stimulating your creative brain.

Once you know how to create Mind Maps, you can gather, on a single page, detailed information on your particular product or service from trade publications, magazines, customers and other sources. Mind Map your key customers to strengthen your client base. Your sales will take off as your customers and your peers come to regard you as the QIP for the information age, the sales expert.

Tony has spent the last 30 years developing and refining this amazing piece of 'brain software' which allows you to become an instant expert on the subjects of your choice – to ensure you are E-QIP-ED for the information age!

You have come a long way. You are gaining insights into how your magnificent brain works. By now you may have realized that the mind–body connection is critical to your sales success. The concept of 'a healthy mind and a healthy body' leads us on to the next chapter.

Skill Builder 30: Mind Maps review

On a separate piece of blank paper, Mind Map this chapter 'Mind Maps'. You may look back.

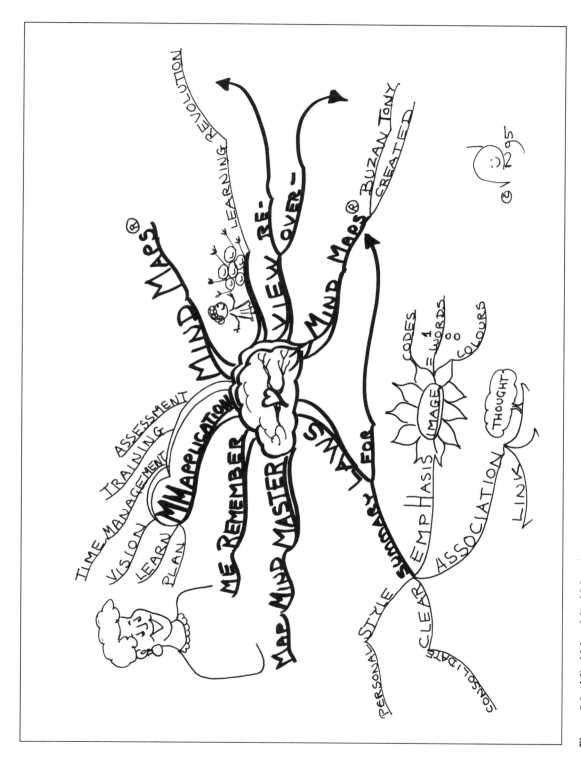

Figure 5.8 Mind Map: Mind Mapping

6 Insight

The mind–body connection

Your greatest prize

Imagine finding in your post one day a letter which informs you that you entered a lottery some time ago and that you have won the first prize – a 1931 Bugatti Royale, worth $8 000 000 and the most expensive car in the world! Some ten days later the prize arrives. All your neighbours and friends gather to see it. There is great excitement as you sign the papers and take proud possession of the most costly car in the world. As the newspaper cameras flash on your beaming face, a reporter asks you where you will keep your new treasure. You explain that you have found a fortified warehouse which has 24-hour security. You have arranged for a team of expert motor mechanics to inspect and service the Bugatti every three weeks. You have taken out a special insurance policy. You are having a unique cover made to keep any damaging light or moisture from reaching its gleaming surface. You explain that this is your most prized possession ... or is it?

How about your mind and your body? What is your mind and your body worth? And how have you been looking after both of them lately? What are you doing about their maintenance, insurance and protection? As you ponder these questions, you wish you had some answers and, guess what? The answers are in this next exciting chapter of *Brain Sell* ... so read on!

Overview

For peak performance you need to understand the mind–body connection and how to keep both in tip-top order. You will soon be both mentally and physically fit for your new, rewarding sales career. A lifetime of sales achievements, satisfied customers and an exciting profession all lie ahead.

The right packaging

If you stop by Barney's in New York, the world's largest men's clothing store, you may meet John Wolohojian, the general manager. While all the salesmen at Barney's are dressed immaculately, Wolohojian looks as though he has just stepped out of the pages of *Gentlemen's Quarterly* magazine. From his finely pressed navy pinstripe suit to his stylish shoes, from his solid gold cufflinks to his tasteful silk tie, Wolohojian projects elegance.

Like all top sales producers, Wolohojian knows how to use his clothing as a tool to increase his sales. By wearing the finest quality suits, shirts and accessories, he immediately establishes himself as an authority on men's clothing, and his customers respect his suggestions for them.

A carpenter or a plumber carries wrenches, hammers and screwdrivers to work every day, and you, too, need certain tools to make your sales job easier. A proper wardrobe is just one of your tools of the trade. You may not work in a clothing store, but how you dress can make an important difference in your customers' response to you. Just as a lawyer carries a briefcase and a physician wears a white coat, your clothing needs to fit in with the message you send your customers. If you are selling hair care products, you need a stylish hairstyle. If you are selling a financial service, you must dress conservatively.

Your personal packaging is one of your essential tools. Customers form their first impressions based on your physical appearance, and those first impressions tend to last, and influence the next steps. Before leaving home in the morning take a moment to glance in the mirror and check your appearance. Ask yourself, 'Do I look my best?' If your hair, face, shoes or clothing don't check out, make the changes before you leave. Remember, you are an extension of the image your company projects.

Wearing the right clothes can also make a difference to how you feel about yourself. Putting on a freshly laundered dress shirt or applying a touch of extra make-up in the morning can improve your self-confidence.

And when you feel good about yourself, your customers will sense it and feel good about buying from you.

Body talk

When you introduce yourself to a customer for the first time, you make an instant and lasting impression. The customer forms that first impression based on your body language, posture, movement, gestures and eye contact, and also from your clothes and grooming.

Your body language can either send a message of self-confidence or disinterest. Swaying from foot to foot, playing with a pen, chewing gum or avoiding eye contact sends a message of 'stay away from me'. If your body language and gestures betray that you are distracted or anxious, it's unlikely that you'll be able to connect with your customer. Good body language involves a balanced posture, holding eye contact, openness and an interested facial expression.

Research suggests that more than half of a sales presentation's impact is determined by the presenter's posture, gestures and eye contact, and almost as much again by voice tone and inflection. That leaves very little scope for the content of the presentation! Evidently, your actions speak overwhelmingly louder than words. So, correct body language and use of voice are essential to sales success.

The mind–body link

For many years it was believed that standing erect, like a soldier, was the correct body posture. However, this stiff and tense appearance is not correct: in fact, the body functions at its best when all its parts are in balance with one another. This results in a release of tensions and smooth flowing movements.

In order to achieve this you need a mind–body awareness of how you use and think about your body in everyday life. Once you relearn how to be balanced, to move more freely and easily you will look and feel better and have more energy, which is critical when you are on your feet and selling all day.

Yes, we did say 'relearn', because the ways in which you are presently holding yourself, walking, standing and acting are habits and patterns that you have learned over a lifetime and, in many cases, learned incorrectly. For the following Skill Builders you will need a full-length mirror, so that you can view your whole self, from your head to your toes.

Skill Builder 31: getting in touch

Read these instructions first and then do the activity. Stand in front of a full-length mirror and observe yourself. Get a sense of yourself as a total person. Become aware of the feelings in your body. Do nothing but observe. This is simply an awareness exercise which can take up to five minutes. As you check out each part of your body from head to toe, do you feel any tension? Look at your face, how does it appear? Relaxed? Tired? Smiling? Or anxious? Your head, is it tilted to one side? Your neck, is it slanted, pushed forwards, or backwards? Your shoulders, are they rounded, level or hiked up? Your ribs, are they jutting forward or rigid? Your stomach, is it sticking out, or pulled in? Your arms, are they bent at the elbows, level, swinging, or tense? Your feet, are they pointed out, straight, balanced, or moving? Take time to *only* observe. Do not make any changes: you are simply getting in touch with yourself.

This is a revealing exercise for many of us who have never been aware of how we really look! You are now using your mind intellectually to observe your body, making the all important mind– body link.

Your brain may be located in your head but it is also controlling your body, sending out a constant stream of messages which can be seen by observing your body. Remember, you are moving all the time; even when you are seated, there are small movements occurring in your body.

Ideally, you want to be balanced. In other words your brain should feel balanced in your body. There are giveaway signals which betray when a brain is not balanced, or suffering from stress – watch a person's feet, for example! If their feet are constantly moving, rocking, shifting weight from side to side, or fidgeting, their brain is sending out a distress signal. As most people are not aware of this they do nothing about it. You now are becoming aware of the body, its movement and its messages. Now you need to practise being balanced.

Skill Builder 32: balanced resting stance

Read all these instructions first and then do the activity. One of the ways to improve your natural posture is to practise the 'balanced resting stance' for a few minutes each day. Stand in front of a full-length mirror, feet shoulder-width apart and arms by your side. Imagine there is a string attached to your head and fixed to the ceiling above, keeping your whole body straight and aligned. Look in the mirror for feedback, then just stand quietly and feel your body's balance. Body balance starts with your feet. If your feet are constantly rocking and moving, your brain is sending out the wrong message.

You are now starting to observe yourself as if you were a third party. This is an important process in the mind–body link. Merely being aware of your brain studying your body is the first step in the process towards change. Observe your balanced resting stance for a few minutes several times each day.

Skill Builder 33: look back in

Read these instructions first and then do the activity. Stand in front of your mirror and get into the balanced resting stance as described in Skill Builder 32. Now start a conversation with yourself about yourself (a subject you should know well!). Maintain eye contact, as you observe yourself. Talk to yourself for a few minutes. Observe your mannerisms. Are you smiling? Are you able to articulate your thoughts freely and coherently without abrupt stops and pauses? Do your facial expressions match your words? Is your body congruent with your message? Does your body change shape as you progress into your talk? What are your feet doing? What are your hands doing? Do not pass judgement; simply observe yourself.

You are now developing your mind–body consciousness. This might well be a very new experience for you – you might even feel that you are meeting a complete stranger for the first time! That's understandable, as, most of your life, you have been experiencing yourself as looking outwards at the world. Now you are looking back in at yourself. Remember, awareness is the first crucial step towards permanent change.

Electrical impulses are firing constantly in your brain. Think of this electricity being used throughout your body as you extend your mind–body connection. Electricity is simply a series of charges, one charge followed by another and then another. You can start to be aware of, and tune into, this current of energy in our next exercise.

Another component of body language is the hand gestures which you use when talking with a customer. Gestures can emphasize or detract from your words. Your gestures should be natural, expressive, clear and congruent with your verbal message. Pointing to a diagram in a brochure

Skill Builder 34: impulses out

Read these instructions first and then do the activity. Stand, with your arms by side, about five feet in front of the mirror. Take a few moments to become aware of yourself. Balance your brain by balancing your feet. Once you are comfortable do not move your feet again. Maintain eye contact with yourself. Then slowly raise your right arm until it is at shoulder height, level and pointing towards the mirror with the palm facing upwards. Hold it there for a few seconds then, letting all the energy drain out, release the arm so that it falls limply back against the side of your body. Repeat the process with your left arm.

Do this with alternate hands about twenty times. Make sure that, when you drop the hand back to its original position by your side, it's fully relaxed so that it makes a slapping sound as it hits your side. As you do this Skill Builder, imagine an electric current flowing through your arm as you raise it. The current is released as you drop the arm.

This exercise, known as 'getting your impulses out' is a favourite in our workshops around the world. Participants enjoy rapid positive results in their speech patterns, confidence levels and self esteem.

Figure 6.1   Impulses

you're describing, so the customer can see it better is an example of the congruent use of hand gestures.

Playing with your hair, tapping your foot, or fiddling with change in your pocket, however, send messages of impatience or nervousness. Customers find these gestures annoying and, however good your verbal presentation, will probably react more negatively to your sales conversation.

One of the finest ways to check your body language and gestures is to videotape yourself in a selling situation. If you don't own a video camera, borrow one from a family member or friend, then have a friend film you or use a tripod to film yourself. Keep the videotape and review it occasionally. In the meantime, work on the areas you wish to improve and film yourself again in a few months to check the results. The following Skill Builder provides a constructive method of doing this.

Skill Builder 35: sales talk

With the videotape rolling, make a five-minute sales talk, either directly to the camera or to a friend acting as the customer. Talk about a product or service you normally sell, and, if possible, have the item present because this will add to your flow of words and ideas.

If you can't get hold of a video camera, the next best thing is to make a sales presentation to a friend. Prepare a checklist beforehand so that your friend knows what to look for: posture, gestures, body movement and eye contact. Use the checklist yourself when reviewing your video playback. (If you can't video, a tape recording is still helpful.)

Reviewing the videotape is a powerful learning experience. No matter how well you think you are projecting yourself, with good observation you can always be improved! This Skill Builder uses all the mental skills of your Sales Mind Matrix.

Tick the appropriate column	Good	Average	Needs Work	Comments
Eye contact				
Posture				
Confidence level				
Energy level				
Use of customer's name				
Body movement				
Dress				
Clarity of explanation				
Gestures				
Knowledge of subject				
Sales Mind Matrix				
Salesenses				
Focused				
Speech – understandable				
Voice – interesting				

Figure 6.2 Checklist for the last four feet

After you have watched the video or listened to your friend's critique, the next step is to improve your gestures, energy level, body movement, posture, and eye contact. These next two self-improvement Skill Builders are fun, and will help you do this.

Skill Builder 36: gibberish

Stand in front of a mirror and spend two or three minutes talking gibberish using your hands to express your thoughts. This turns off your intellectual brain while your intuitive brain concentrates on the gestures. Young children play this game with total ease and enjoyment – and so can you. This Skill Builder is highly effective in eliminating shyness.

Skill Builder 37: silent sale

This powerful and enjoyable Skill Builder involves practising a totally silent sales conversation, relying solely on gestures. Since our bodies do a good deal of the communicating, this is an ideal way to develop this skill.

Stand in front of a mirror, video camera or friend and spend two or three minutes communicating without words. Use only your hands and body to express your thoughts. As you proceed with the mental conversation, your brain will find creative ways to communicate. Again, use the videotape, mirror or friend for feedback.

These last seven Skill Builders are designed to improve your mind–body connection as well as to develop that considerable impact that your body posture, gestures and eye contact has on your sales presentation. The next area we want you to work on is your voice. Remember that your voice tone and inflection accounts for over a third of the impact of your sales presentation.

Voice power

Imagine watching the nightly news on television and listening to an announcer who keeps slurring his words or mumbling. How long would you be attentive if you couldn't understand what was said?

As a salesperson, your voice is one of your most important trade tools. Like the TV announcer, you are in the communication business. The sound of your voice has a powerful effect on your customers.

Skill Builder 38: voice power

Now is the time to take out a tape recorder. Ask a friend to act as the customer and decide the product or service to be sold. Make certain that he or she has some specific needs to make the sale realistic. Keep the conversation going for four to five minutes. You might need to try this more than once to get a good recording. When you have finished the recording, save it so that you can analyse it later.

Play back and listen to your sales presentation and note all the words and expressions which might annoy your customer or reduce the impact of the presentation. Consider noting the number of uses of annoying expressions which may have become so much a part of our normal speech that we hardly realize we're using them. 'You know', 'uhmms' or 'uhhs' are prime examples.

Listening to your voice for the first time can be stressful, as it might not sound as you imagined it to be – so be prepared for this.

On the tape, your voice should be clear, natural and expressive. Note the speed of your speech. Many salespeople speak too quickly because they are nervous. You can gain control by taking in a deep breath and letting it out to the count of five.

You can improve your speech dramatically with one simple technique – learning to pause. Speech without pauses is like reading without full stops. Each time you pause, you attract your customer's attention and interest. Pauses give your customer time to understand what you are saying and give you time to think of what you are going to say next!

How about the tone of your voice? Listen to the tape recording again – does your voice sound interesting or monotonous? An intriguing voice will keep your customer's attention, and having a distinctive voice means that the moment you call your customer on the phone, he or she will remember you, even before you mention your name.

Just as no one in school taught you to listen well, chances are no one showed you how to use your voice correctly. The next two Skill Builders, which both use all the mental skills from your Sales Mind Matrix, will improve the quality of your speech.

Skill Builder 39: the energy scale

First, count slowly from one to ten, then backwards from ten to one. Now do this again, but start with a whisper on one and raise the volume until you say ten as loudly as you can without shouting or straining. Known as moving up the energy scale, it gives each number more vocal energy as you progress. Next, count down from ten to one, starting loud at ten and ending in a whisper at one. Practise this Skill Builder for a few minutes a day for 14 days. Raising and lowering your volume is essential to effective speaking. It provides more control over your voice and makes your speech more interesting to your customers.

Skill Builder 40: tape it

For the second Skill Builder, read aloud an article from the daily newspaper or a magazine into a tape recorder or to a friend. As you read the article, vary your speech and make it sound as appealing as possible. Think of the meaning of each word and phrase and pronounce it clearly so that your listener understands. Ask yourself if your delivery should be slow or fast, loud or soft, or with a rhythm. What about the tone of your voice? Do this Skill Builder as frequently as possible over the next month, because it will dramatically improve your everyday speech.

Figure 6.3   Tape it!

Training Olympic sales athletes

For years Tony has been successfully training Olympic athletes on how to use their Sales Mind Matrix to win their athletic events. He is an adviser to international Olympic coaches and athletes and to the British Olympic rowing squads as well as to the British chess teams. You can also train, in the same way, to become an 'Olympic sales athlete'.

With 'Olympic' training, each time you enter *the last four feet* you will give the best performance of your life. You need to have a healthy body and mind to operate at your best level. Top sales producers know that physical and mental health go hand-in-hand on the path to success. There are several time-tested ways to improve the link between your mind and body which, practised regularly, will give you more balance and reduce the daily stress in your life.

The importance of the mind–body connection was first emphasized by the ancient Greeks, who taught us that a healthy mind resulted in a healthy body. As a successful sales person, you surely need a healthy body, as you rely on your body to work at its best each day you sell. If you have a car that breaks down, just think how it disrupts your life. The same applies to your body. The ancient Greeks also knew that the mind and the body were interlinked – that the body relied on the mind and the mind relied on the body so they both needed to be healthy.

Healthy lifestyle

Getting enough sleep and exercising regularly are both essential to a healthy lifestyle. Going to bed at a regular time also programmes you to fall asleep quickly. Brief catnaps during the day are also highly recommended as they give you time to daydream and give your brain a chance to integrate much of what has happened in the preceding few hours. As a Skill Builder you should join a health club or buy a workout videotape and develop a healthy lifestyle.

Little me

Within each one of us is a small barometer, a 'little me' that changes according to our moods. When the barometer goes up, you hear a little voice inside say 'I feel great today'. When it goes down, the voice asks, 'When are we going to have some fun?' You should tune into this voice and take time for fun and relaxation. Working hard and achieving goals is fine, but you also need to celebrate your successes, otherwise you will exhaust yourself, and have to contend with stress and burnout.

Skill Builder 41: little me

The object of this Skill Builder is to get in touch with your 'little me' and to know what it wants as a reward.

Figure 6.4   Little me

Take a moment to Mind Map, on a separate sheet of paper, all the enjoyable things you like to do. Some examples may be:

- taking a bubble bath
- riding a bicycle
- building sandcastles on the beach
- going to a movie
- having a meal in a restaurant.

Once you have a series of ideas, choose the best three, and next to each one, write down the date when you intend to do the activity. Enter the dates in your diary and then complete them, to prove to your 'little me' that you mean business!

Next time you hear that little voice inside ask, 'When are we going to have some more fun?', look up your Mind Map and carve out a chunk of time for the things you enjoy. Remember, it's never too late for the child within you to have some fun. Even more importantly, fun, relaxation and other personal endeavours are Sales Mind Matrix activities that supply you with a balanced lifestyle.

Breath of life

The next consideration is to take conscious control of your breathing. This will help you stay energized, focused and relaxed throughout your day.

Notice how you are breathing now. Are your breaths coming from high in your chest or are your breathing deeply from your diaphragm? Your diaphragm is a muscular membrane, like a big tent that separates your abdominal and thoracic cavities. Place both hands over your stomach and see whether your hands move with each breath. If the hands don't move, you are breathing in your chest; if they do move, you are breathing from you diaphragm.

When tense, you tend to breathe from your chest. When relaxed, you breathe more deeply from your diaphragm. When you are sleeping at night and are totally relaxed, you automatically change to deep diaphragm breathing. This increases the oxygen taken into the bloodstream and carried to the muscles, giving you more energy. By learning to inhale deeply in the daytime, your breathing becomes slower and more self-composed, calming your nerves, steadying your emotions and relaxing the body.

Imagine that, in the middle of a hectic day with all your new customers and business, you find that you are becoming stressed and uptight. Wouldn't it be wonderful if you could somehow stay calm and relaxed, and take control of your emotions? You can do that by practising the 'complete breath', explained in the next Skill Builder.

Skill Builder 42: techniques for relaxation

The objective of the 'complete breath' is to give you an instant technique for relaxing yourself at any time and in any place. There are two methods, both of which are explained below.

Method A

Begin taking the air in slowly through your nose. Then push your diaphragm down, so that the air can enter the lower part of your lungs. When you have filled the lower part of your lungs, continue to inhale. Expand your chest as much as possible, allowing the air to enter the high area of the lungs. Hold the breath to the count of five, then exhale deeply, relaxing your shoulders and chest and contracting your diaphragm to expel all the air from your lungs.

Hint: Close your eyes while breathing and imagine breathing energy – give it a yellow colour. As you breathe out, imagine all the nervous tension and energy leaving your body in a red stream.

Method B

Another technique is to breath in through your nose, then close your eyes and tense all the muscles in your body, from clenched fists to clenched toes, while holding your breath, for about ten seconds. Then relax at the same time as you let the air out of your lungs. Do this exercise another once or twice, and notice the difference in how you feel.

Learning the complete breath takes a little practice, but within a few days this technique will become second nature.

Renewed energy

Do you know how to relax while at work? This doesn't mean losing interest or leaving work early – it means running a mind movie that allows you to relax for two or three minutes and then return to your work with renewed energy and enthusiasm.

The following Skill Builder shows you how to do this.

Skill Builder 43: mind movie

Find a quiet place where you won't be interrupted, sit down, close your eyes, take a deep breath and then breathe out. On the next in-breath imagine the air going down through your legs, filling your feet and toes. Hold the breath for a few moments, then breathe out through your mouth and imagine all the nervous tension leaving your toes.

On your next in-breath, picture the air filling both legs. Hold the breath, then exhale through your mouth, imagining all the nervous tension leaving your legs. Take the next breath down into your stomach and thighs, hold it as it collects all the nervous tension and then let it out through your mouth. On your next four breaths, do the same with your chest, both hands and fingers, both arms, and lastly your shoulders, neck and head.

By this time you will have released most of the nervous tension in your body. Breathe in deeply again, letting the air fill your whole body, hold it and then, as you breathe out, you will get rid of all the remaining nervous tension.

> Practise this relaxation technique at home a few times. Then you can use it any time during your workday and enjoy all its benefits.

Your mental bank account

Like breathing, your thinking is an automatic process that continues day after day with a never-ending stream of thoughts. Your thousands of thoughts are like a mental bank account – each day you have a positive or negative balance that carries over to the next day. If you usually have a negative balance, you slowly become an unhappy person, whose glass is always half-empty instead of half-full.

A typical salesperson lets others influence his or her thinking. A co-worker who tells you business is bad will create negative thoughts in your mind, a difficult customer may upset you, and one unfortunate event can make you feel bad all day. However, you can take control of your thoughts just as easily as you took control of your breathing. You can consciously create the positive thoughts you want. This will change your behaviour and improve your sales performance.

If you want to become a high producer, then you must take control of your thoughts. A positive thinker will outperform a negative thinker every day. *You* are responsible for your thoughts, so take charge and watch your sales climb!

Thought control

Can you take control of your thoughts? Yes, you can! You can gain conscious control over your thoughts, just as you did with your breathing.

Most people have thousands of thoughts every day. How many of these thoughts do you control – a dozen or two? Without direction, your thoughts will wander in any direction they choose. Generally, your thoughts will either be positive or negative. Each positive or negative thought affects your body causing relaxation or stress, enthusiasm or lack of interest, or a good or bad feeling about yourself. Your thoughts show in how you walk and talk, how you treat your customers, how you treat yourself, and in your sales results.

First, become conscious of your thoughts – become an impartial third party and simply observe them. This technique takes practice, as the tendency is to get 'hooked' by thoughts and become carried away – often by thoughts you don't really want to be party to!

New mental images

When you notice thoughts not to your liking, the secret is not to give them any energy, which makes them stronger in your mind, but to replace them with positive, beautiful, inspiring, or constructive thoughts. You should have a series of these thoughts ready, so that you can 'plug them in' when you need to.

Taking control of your thoughts is a process of changing your mental images for the better. For example, if you 'see' yourself as clumsy with customers, then that's how you will behave while selling. If you picture yourself as confident, knowledgeable and helpful to your customers, and realistically working towards that goal, you will be.

These mental pictures, or inner models have real power. Over the long term, they shape who you are. Do you 'see' and 'hear' and 'feel' yourself as a positive or negative person? You have the power to change your world for the better simply by developing positive new pictures and new sound-tracks.

Skill Builder 44: thought analyser

With *you* as the central image, Mind Map, on a separate sheet of paper, *all* the thoughts you remember having over the last 24 hours. As you work on the Mind Map you will keep adding more and more thoughts. Then choose a colour for negative thoughts and one for positive thoughts – and colour the Mind Map. Finally, analyse what triggered those negative thoughts. Was it something that someone else said or did?

Skill Builder 45: the new you

Find a quiet spot and sit down and relax. Then picture yourself in the future. Once you have created a strong, positive mental picture of yourself (an 'inner model') see how you could make that mental future 'you' more successful. Imagine yourself as confident and equipped with all the most up-to-date knowledge about your product or service.

In this way, you are using your Sales Mind Matrix, your salesenses, and your truth-seeking brain to create a successful inner model of you! Next, make the mental future picture three-dimensional and in full colour. Add bright lights and your favourite upbeat music to this inner model. (For more details see Part One, Chapter 3 on SMASHIN' SCOPE.)

Practise this inner modelling Skill Builder until you can visualize yourself instantly as a successful, self-confident salesperson. Once you have achieved this, add the image to your anchor (see Part One, Chapter 2 for more details).

Review

'Insight: the mind–body connection' has given you a good number of Skill Builders which, on reflection, have followed a pattern. The first series dealt with awareness of the mind–body link and the importance of balance. These were followed by a series of Skill Builders to develop your voice. The final Skill Builders concerned keeping your mind–body connection healthy and stress-free, by means of breathing, visualization and thought processing techniques.

Your thoughts are affecting both your mind and your body. However, you can choose the *quality* of your thoughts! This is true transformation – a power within your control, each second of your conscious life. *Choose wisely*.

Give yourself the right direction and be motivated as you move to a healthier 'you', balanced in both mind and body. Be proud of yourself and your progress. Congratulate yourself on taking another significant step in your personal growth and mental development.

Gaining control of your thoughts is continued at a more advanced level in Part Three, 'Turn Customers into Gold'.

Skill Builder 46: insight review

On a separate sheet of blank paper, Mind Map Chapter 6 'Insight'. You may look back.

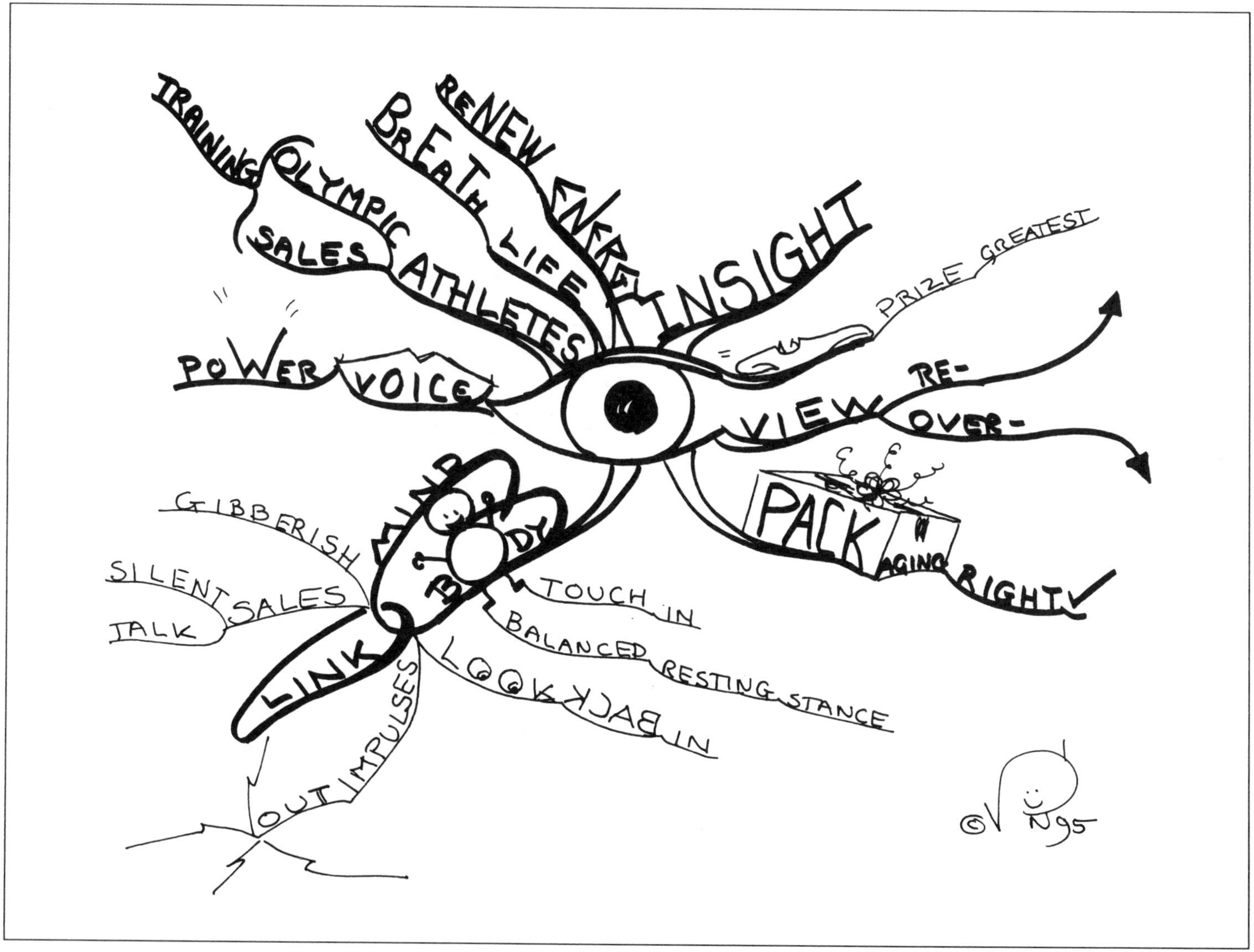

Figure 6.5 Mind Map: insight

PART THREE

Turn customers into gold

Introduction

Brain Sell explains how to become a knowledgeable salesperson who by ensuring that customers get what they want, achieves an increased sales performance. The book explores how your customers' minds work, based on the latest scientific research on the brain and the experiences of some world's top sales producers.

Part One had three chapters. Chapter 1, 'Whole-Brain Selling', introduced the Sales Mind Matrix which comprises the ten different mental skills of your whole creative brain. This led into Chapter 2, 'Salesenses', which dealt with how information enters your brain through your senses and how it is communicated back to your customers' five senses. Chapter 3, 'Memory Imprints', explained how to remember customers' names and faces.

Having understood how to apply your Sales Mind Matrix to all types of sales situations, you moved on to the three chapters of Part Two. Chapter 4, 'Infocentre', gave you the keys to mastering information in the 'information age' and showed you how to think of yourself as 'an information centre' able to answer all your customers' questions on your product or service. Chapter 5, 'Mind Maps', gave you a new whole-brain technique known as Mind Mapping which enables you to absorb and retain large amounts of information. Chapter 6, 'Insight', introduced the mind–body connection, gave insights into how these two parts must work in harmony if you wish to achieve a superior sales performance and showed you how to get your mind and body in perfect shape.

Parts One and Two form the background to Part Three, 'Turn Customers into Gold' which also comprises three chapters. In Chapter 7, 'Mind Search. Discover Your Private Mental Video', you learn how to use your own internal 'video screen' to view your customer's needs. Chapter 8, 'Sales Detective. Develop Super-Sleuth Sales Skills', tells you how, with the aid of sales detective questions and other super-sleuth methods, you will be able to enter your customers' minds and discover their real needs. Never again will you make mistakes about what the customer said or wanted. You will now have the means to accurately assess your customers' needs.

The journey to the completion of the sale is nearly over. You have a clear picture of your customer's needs and are more than ready to satisfy them. The final chapter of Part Three 'The Sales Compass. Give Your Customers What THEY Want', gives the *Brain Sell* approach to gaining a satisfied customer. This means giving your customer whatever he or she wishes. To do this, you simply use the Sales Compass to match your customer's needs precisely with information and products or services. This breakthrough sales technique will act as both a check and a guide to ensure that you are using your whole creative brain in the selling process. Taken a step further, it allows you to analyse any conversation to find out the different mental skills your customer is using. You will begin to understand sales conversations in a totally new light. The result? Satisfied customers who will return to you again and again.

The chapters which follow will show how you can:

● turn words into mental pictures;
● change your brain power into selling power;
● accurately establish your customer's needs;
● rapidly understand what your customers are thinking;
● build a loyal customer base;
● have unlimited *satisfied customers*.

As before, each of the three chapters contain Skill Builders, all designed to help you sell better. Again, to make the best use of Part Three, first skim through it rapidly to get a general understanding, then read it in depth and do all the Skill Builders in the correct sequence. For maximum benefit we recommend that you spend a week on each chapter, giving yourself time for in-depth reading, study, practice time for the Skill Builders and time for your brain to absorb and integrate all the new material into your everyday sales behaviour.

To speed up the mastery of these new materials we strongly recommend that you talk about them to your family, friends and peers at work. If you belong to a club, association or group, make a short presentation on any aspect of the book you wish. This will allow you to practise many skills in the book, and the results will delight you.

7 Mind search

Discover your private mental video screen

X-ray vision

Imagine that you have a special pair of glasses that give you X-ray vision. These glasses can show you your customers' exact needs. Even if the customers are uncertain of their needs, your glasses can probe into the hidden layers of their minds, giving you their images, their words, their emotions, their own logic, their history and their daydreams – the entire mental picture, a multidimensional picture of their needs.

What would such a pair of glasses be worth to you? What would such a pair of glasses do to develop your customer satisfaction? This chapter gives you that X-ray vision.

Overview

This chapter shows you how to turn your Sales Mind Matrix into a private video screening room – to change customer conversations into movies. Changing words into images enables you to form accurate pictures of what your customers want! Selling becomes easy and exciting, with each customer contact opening up unlimited opportunities.

Pick the right words

While working with a team of managers at International Distillers and Vintners (UK) Ltd, Richard asked what they considered was the most important skill that their staff needed in order to improve their productivity. The answer was 'an ability to listen'. 'If only we could teach them to be better listeners!' was a common response.

Why do we have so much difficulty with hearing and understanding what the customer is saying? One reason is that we have learned to listen in the same way as we have learned to read – with only our left cortical skills. As you remember, the left cortex is the side that likes to hear one word at a time in an orderly sequence. That's the way customers speak to you. Yet, while you're listening to each word as it comes out of your customer's mouth, the other half of your brain becomes bored because it doesn't have anything to do. Your attention starts to wander and you become distracted as your right brain thinks about, looks for, or listens to other more interesting things!

And that's not all. Many customers talk and talk, without giving you any information which you could use to advance the sale, while other customers have difficulties in expressing their thoughts.

For example, listen to what one customer might tell you: 'I was looking through the paper this morning, *The Daily Express* – I always read it before breakfast. In the *Daily Express* you had an advertisement for portable computers. My wife decided it was about time I had a portable computer. She's coming in now. I wonder if you could point us in the right direction.'

From a sales point of view, the two key words here are 'portable computers'. That's easy to picture, but look how much talking the customer did – more than 50 words to express one simple idea!

Your know from *Brain Sell*, Part One, that your brain thinks and remembers faster and better when you use pictures (see Chapter 1, 'Sales Mind Matrix', for more details). Because of the way your whole brain works, one picture is worth more than 1000 words. So, you must learn to take the customers' words and turn them into pictures.

Word types

The question is, what are the best words for the pictures and images that will aid recall? Words which often seem quite good at the time do not, for some reason, prove adequate for recall. To explain why, it is necessary to discuss the difference between key recall words and key creative words, and the way in which they interact after a time.

Figure 7.1   Key words

Key recall words

A key recall word or phrase is one which funnels into itself a wide range of information and which, when triggered, funnels back the same picture. It will tend to be an evocative noun or verb associated in the mind with key adjectives or adverbs.

Figure 7.2   Key recall word

Creative words

A creative word is one which is particularly memorable and image-forming, but is far more evocative than the more directed key recall

FANTASTIC

Figure 7.3   Creative word

word. Words like 'wow' and 'weird' are especially memorable but do not necessarily evoke a specific image.

As well as understanding the difference between creative and key recall words, it is also necessary to understand words themselves and the brain which uses them.

'Velcro' words

Many a sale is lost because the words used by the salesperson have a different meaning to the customer and vice versa. In the following example a customer and a salesperson are discussing the merits of buying a new car.

Salesperson: 'This car is a wise investment.'
Customer: 'You mean, it will be worth more in the future?'
Salesperson: 'No, I mean it will be low on maintenance and running costs.'
Customer: 'That's not my understanding of the word "investment"!'

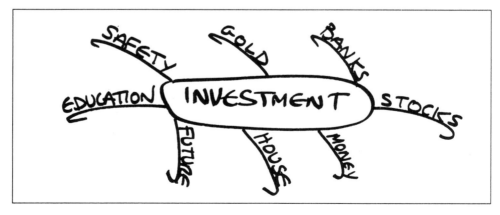

Figure 7.4   Velcro word

It is as if every word is metaphorically covered in Velcro, or covered with little hooks, so that it can easily attach to other words to give both words in the new pair slightly different meanings. In the example above, the word 'investment' is hooked quite differently in 'low on maintenance and running costs' and 'will be worth more in the future'.

Experience this for yourself in our next Skill Builder.

Skill Builder 47: Velcro word

For the following Velcro word, 'money', complete the hooks by writing in the different meanings 'money' has for you. Then, ask your friends or colleagues to do the same exercise and compare how you differ.

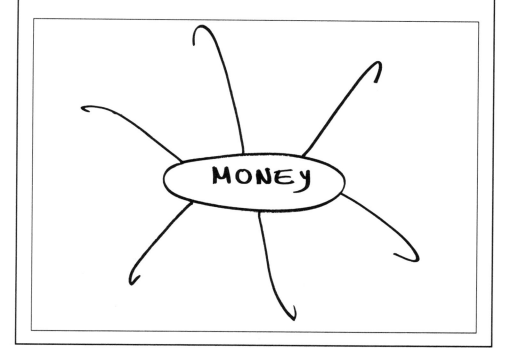

It takes two to tango

In addition to having its own Velcro words, each person's brain is different. When selling, in *the last four feet* the customer is part of your experience as a salesperson and, equally, you are part of the customer's experience. It takes two to tango! Because the associations that you have will therefore be different from those experienced by the customer, it becomes increasingly important to clarify both the words you are using and those the customer is using in order to establish common ground and mutual understanding.

Absorbing your customer

Now that you understand the Velcro, sensory nature of words, and the 15 mental thought processes of your Sales Mind Matrix, you can appreciate that, to listen effectively, you have to understand information as it enters the brain in terms of every word, every number, every line, every colour, every smell, every touch and every picture. You have to comprehensively absorb your customer's mental, physical and general being. When your Sales Mind Matrix is active in this process your attention will no longer wander.

3-D mind movie

To remember clearly what your customers say, create pictures in your mind, turning their words into clear mental images. Mental images or 'brain pictures' include all the multi-ordinate, multi-hooked nature of words and the multisensory nature of information. This gives a new dimension to listening. It's as though each word creates a 3-D movie in your mind. As you listen to your customers, focus your whole creative brain on hearing one key idea in order to create your own brain picture of what he or she wants.

Start with one image

When you listen in words, it's easy to miss the nuggets of gold emerging from your customer's mouth. And it's easy to forget what your customer said five minutes, and 5000 words ago. But when you are listening in 'brain pictures', you don't have to remember all 5000 words. You need a strong central image or key word to start your brain picture, then you must keep adding to it. For example, the customer might say: 'I want my home to be totally secure.' What strong central images come to mind?

Turning words into brain pictures

Once you have that central image, you can ask questions and keep adding to that image until you have a complete brain picture. For instance, once you have a brain picture of the portable computer, you could ask your customer such questions as:

- 'What make did you have in mind?'
- 'How much memory do you require?'
- 'Do you want a colour screen?'
- 'Do you have a computer now?'
- 'Will you need a computer case?'

Customers do know

However, if a customer gives you little or no information as regards his or her central image do not construct one. You can't create a mental picture of something you haven't heard or seen. In such a situation, ask your customer, 'What did you have in mind?' and then wait for an answer as the customer does a mental sweep, looking for the right image or picture. Remain silent while waiting for the customer to answer – if you interrupt her train of thought you will be unlikely to get an answer! Most customers *do* know what they want, and it's your job to help them express their real needs.

Listen, listen, listen

Of course, not all customers are clear in their communications. Think how frustrated you would be if your customer said, 'Well, I was sick yesterday and I'm not feeling very good today. Does anyone have a handkerchief? Thank you. Now where was I? Oh yes. I think I would like to give you an order but I left the details in my other office. My memory is just not what it should be. Ever since I lost my parrot I've had trouble remembering. Did you see the show on television last night, about South America? I thought it was terrific. Oh, I forgot to tell you about the special offer at the supermarket. If you like chickens they've got a great deal.'

By this time, you probably would have created brain pictures of handkerchiefs, an order, parrots, South America and chickens!

As you won't be able to teach your customers how to express themselves more clearly, it is best to learn to listen in pictures. Listen for clues about the central image, then keep asking questions to develop it. Keep your mind focused, don't be distracted, and listen, listen, listen.

Imaging warm-ups

To develop the skill of listening in brain pictures, you must first practise rapidly forming brain pictures. Remember, everyone can do it. The following Skill Builders will help you to develop the technique.

Skill Builder 48: bedroom scene

Think about your bedroom. Mentally describe it to yourself, as you go around the room. What are the colours? Are there pictures on the wall? Describe your bed. Do you have a reading lamp? As you look around your bedroom, you will surprised at the details you uncover, and you will find your own unique way to create your brain pictures.

Next, when you have the chance, go into your real bedroom and check to see how accurate your brain pictures were! Go slowly around the room and look for the details you might have missed in your mental picture.

Then develop another brain picture of your bedroom. This time you will get much more detail. Again, check out your brain picture against the physical bedroom.

Keep repeating this process until the mental picture is close to reality.

Skill Builder 49: recent purchase

Read through the instructions before starting the activity.
Mentally re-create your last important purchase.

- What was it?
- Where did you buy it?
- Why did you buy it?
- How much was it?
- Who sold it to you?
- How did you pay for it?
- Have you used it yet?
- Are you pleased with it?

This exercise will help you to develop your brain picture skills.

Skill Builder 50: a journey

Read through the instructions before you start the activity.

Close your eyes and think of how you would go from where you are now to the nearest airport. What form of transport would you use? How far is it? What sounds and smells would you experience? What other traffic, people, sights would you experience? As you take the imaginary journey, you are again developing your skill of thinking in brain pictures.

Develop your own brain pictures

Now you have observed that, with a little practice, you could rapidly develop this skill of thinking in brain pictures, the next three Skill Builders give you three different customer conversations for practice. As you read each one, form a central mental image in your mind and start adding to it. Use words or your own code to develop your own brain pictures.

Skill Builder 51: develop a brain picture A

Customer: 'I wanted to give my wife a 50th birthday present. I was thinking of taking her for a week to Europe. She loves historic cities and I thought of London, Rome or Paris. I want this to be a first-class trip, from travel, to hotels, to tours.'

Skill Builder 52: develop a brain picture B

Customer: 'I'm considering redecorating my kitchen. I want white tiles throughout with strip neon lighting in the ceiling. I want a new fridge, stove and dishwasher all built in. The sink needs to be replaced and I want the floor to be light oakwood. I need wine racks built in one corner for my 200 bottles of wine.'

Skill Builder 53: develop a brain picture C

> *Customer*: 'I want a morning-only job within 20 miles of my home. I am a fully certified nurse and trained to work in the operating theatre. I am prepared to work weekends and public holidays. I have specialized training in working with babies and children up to 12 years of age.'

Notice how easy it is to create mental images when your customers can express clearly exactly what they want.

Four key principles

The four important principles that help you to develop brain pictures of your customers' conversations:

1. Stay open.
2. Stay in the present.
3. Listen for nouns.
4. Use your Sales Mind Matrix.

Let's consider each one of these important principles in detail.

Stay open

Making a negative judgement while listening to a customer is a common mistake. When you say to yourself, 'This customer won't buy' or 'This is wasting my time' or 'This is a pain', you will tune out and you won't get a clear picture from your customer's words.

Suppose, while listening to your customer ask for a new kitchen, you thought to yourself, 'This person can't afford this type of kitchen'. Once you had made that judgement, you would probably stop listening to her.

Being judgemental is a bad habit. To break it, you must monitor your own thinking. While your customer is talking, practise turning his words into pictures. The next Skill Builder develops your ability to listen in brain pictures without making judgements.

Skill Builder 54: stay open

Read the following description of a situation and then create a brain picture of what the customer is looking for.

You make an appointment with a customer to sell a home security system, but arrive 15 minutes late. The customer says: 'Well, it's about time you appeared. You people are never on time. I suppose you're too busy to really worry about a little person like me. My home needs to be wired for intruders and I'm just too scared to leave it at night. I can't leave my cats at home all alone and unprotected. Are you going to advise me what systems to have, or are you just too busy?'

How did you do? Do not fall into the trap of getting emotionally hooked by this type of conversation. Build brain pictures of what the customer wants. In the above example, your central image is 'home alarm system'. Once you have this central image, you can start developing the complete brain picture by asking questions related to it.

Stay in the present

Listening to a customer chatter on and on can be boring, or sometimes nervewracking or stressful. But, if you allow your mind to wander, you stop listening and will probably miss important information. 'Staying in the present' means constantly being aware of your customer's actions and statements.

Often, when you are listening to a conversation one word can trigger a completely new line of thought in your own mind, preventing you from concentrating on the customer's actual words.

Let's go back to our portable computer example. When the customer said, 'I was looking through the paper this morning' the word 'paper' might start you thinking, 'Oh, I must read the paper tonight. Will we win the football game?' At this point you have started thinking about what might happen in the future and have stopped listening to your customer in the present.

Alternatively, the word 'paper' might have sent you off on another direction: 'Wonder if I've thrown away last Sunday's paper – there was that article I wanted to cut out and save.' Again, you have lost touch with your customer's words and are now thinking about the past. To create a clear brain picture of what your customer wants, you must end those distractions, stay in the present and concentrate on what's happening now by continuously creating and building your brain pictures.

Skill Builder 55: being present

Find a quiet place where you won't be interrupted. Standing or seated, fix your eyes on any one object in the room. Now hold your attention on that object. It could be a picture, a door, a carpet, anything. If your mind wanders off, direct it back to the chosen object.

If you are able to hold the object in your mind for three minutes, without interruption by other thoughts, you have achieved a remarkable result. Initially you might be able to hold your attention for 15 seconds and then your mind may wander. Keep practising until you can hold the object for a minute or more.

While observing the object, place yourself as an observer. In other words, observe yourself observing the object. You might be surprised at how many different thoughts flow into your mind. The secret is to let these thoughts flow in and out, while you refocus on the object of your choice. This is a powerful Skill Builder for staying in the present.

Skill Builder 56: quick brain pictures

For practice in recognizing nouns, develop a quick brain picture of each of the following:

- A rich, ripe, red, juicy strawberry
- A cruise liner
- An elephant
- A map of the world
- Big Ben
- A football
- A glass of water
- A jet plane taking off
- New office desk
- A plate of spaghetti
- A postage stamp
- A toothbrush
- Blue eyes
- A typewriter
- A barking dog
- A ringing bell.

Listen for nouns

When changing a customer's words into brain pictures, always listen for nouns. It's easy to visualize words like 'portable computer', 'stockbroker' or 'airbus'. With and without accompanying adjectives they help you form a rapid, complete central image.

Use Sales Mind Matrix

Let's look again at the Sales Mind Matrix, shown here in Figure 7.5.

	0%	25%	50%	75%	100%	
Sound						TOTALS
Sight						
Smell						
Taste						
Touch						
Numbers						TOTALS
Words						
Logic						
Lists						
Details						
Pictures						TOTALS
Imagination						
Colour						
Rhythm						
Space						

Figure 7.5   Sales Mind Matrix – complete

Now consider how you can use the Sales Mind Matrix to build your brain pictures. You can use these mental skills to build up your brain

Skill Builder 57: tune in

One fast way to learn, or to increase your skill of, listening is to listen to your radio. As you listen to your favourite news station, see if you can create brain pictures of what is being said. A good radio script is written in a format designed to create pictures in the listener's mind! As you listen, turn the words into a movie.

Use the Sales Mind Matrix in Figure 7.6 to analyse your favourite news station. Listening to a radio news station is a powerful, enjoyable and quick way to learn how to change words into brain pictures. You will have many opportunities to apply this skill builder in the months ahead – use them!

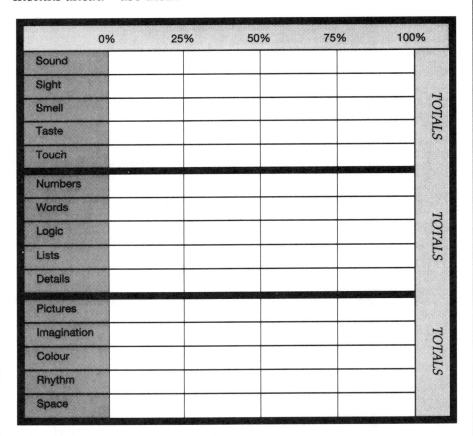

	0%	25%	50%	75%	100%	
Sound						TOTALS
Sight						
Smell						
Taste						
Touch						
Numbers						TOTALS
Words						
Logic						
Lists						
Details						
Pictures						TOTALS
Imagination						
Colour						
Rhythm						
Space						

Figure 7.6   Sales Mind Matrix – complete

pictures, making the pictures stronger and easier to recall. In Part One, Chapter 3, 'Memory Imprints', we covered SMASHIN' SCOPE, the sales memory method based on three keys:

- imagination
- association
- motivation.

Using your Sales Mind Matrix together with SMASHIN' SCOPE gives you an enormous range of mental skills to build rapid, complete and memorable brain pictures.

Review

When making your brain picture, apply the four principles:

1. **Stay open.** Judgements have a way of distorting reality and can work against you.
2. **Stay in the present.** Your mind tends to wander. If you allow yourself to follow your roving mind, you lose your concentration. Be aware of your mind and the games it plays.
3. **Listen for nouns.** They inspire rapid mental pictures and help you create that central image. From that central image you can start branching out.
4. **Use your Sales Mind Matrix and SMASHIN' SCOPE.** This enormous range of mental skills builds rich brain pictures.

These four principles will help you develop excellent, memorable and complete brain pictures.

When turning your customer's conversation into brain pictures, remember that this forms an internal Mind Map on your internal video screen. Once you have developed this new mental skill, you will be ready to take on a new intriguing role in the sales process – that of a sales detective! You will be searching for clues, observing, listening, using your Sales Mind Matrix, all designed to complete those brain pictures and resulting in *satisfied customers*!

Skill Builder 58: Mind search review

> On a separate piece of blank paper, Mind Map this chapter 'Mind Search'. You may look back.

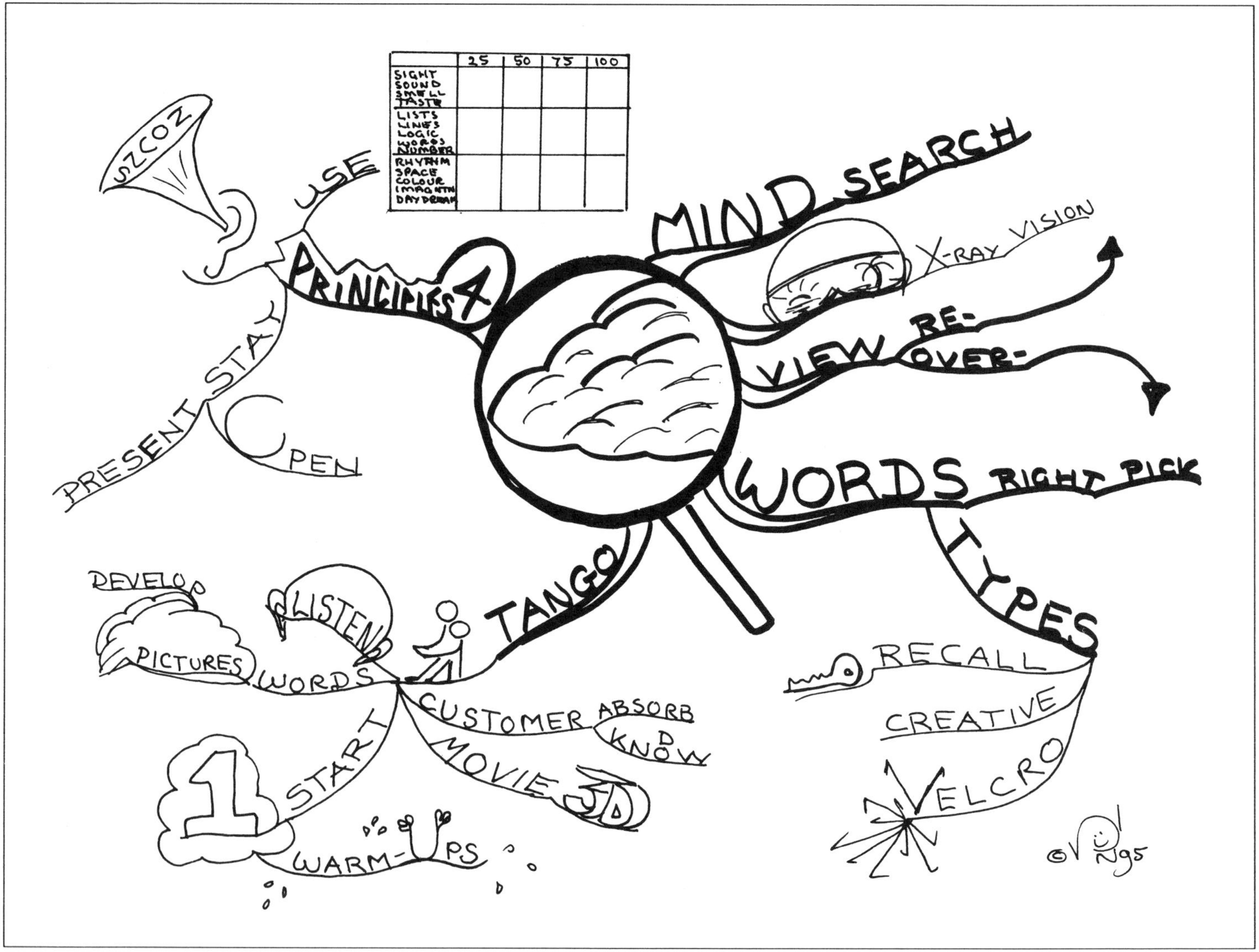

Figure 7.7 Mind Map: mind search

8　Sales detective

Develop super-sleuth sales skills

The magic badge

Imagine that when you go to work today you find that each potential customer is wearing a little magic badge around their neck. Displayed on that badge, in wonderful colours and in the finest detail, is a Mind Map of the products or services they need to buy from you!

The central image is of the actual item or service they wish to purchase. Branching off from the central image are all the details. There are major branches for the key requirements – colour, size, and quality – and separate branches for the price point, delivery date and reasons for purchase.

All you need to do now is match your customer's Mind Map with the actual product and service and you have a satisfied customer, a sale and a growing client base. Would this magical badge of your customer's internal pictures, in Mind Map form, make selling easy and fun? Of course it would! Just imagine what would happen to your sales! You would be able to satisfy every customer you met! You would be the Super Salesperson. Articles about you would appear in magazines and newspapers. You would address sales conventions on your amazing abilities. You would become a legend in your own lifetime!

On the other hand, why bother to imagine all this when you can make it happen now? Simply study the material in this chapter, 'The Sales Detective' – your next step to success.

Overview

From this chapter you will learn sales detective skills, including questions, which will help complete a clear brain picture of your customer's needs on your internal video. You will put on your super-sleuth hat and hunt for sales clues. This chapter will transform selling into an exciting detective game, and it's fun!

Super-sleuth

Detective questions

We think of a detective as a person who solves a mystery, someone who finds the missing pieces to jigsaw puzzles. This is the role you must assume. Think of the complete picture of what the customer wants to buy as a fragmented jigsaw puzzle. Once you have put together the complete picture and matched the product or service you are selling precisely to the customer's jigsaw puzzle (brain picture), you have a satisfied customer.

Your customer's jigsaw puzzle can be solved by the answers to your questions. Each answer is a piece of the puzzle so, like a detective, you have to be skilled in asking the right questions. You are, in effect, a sales detective, searching for clues.

Using your internal video

Once you have learned to listen in pictures and formed a brain picture, you have an accurate idea of your customer's needs.

The first step in creating a brain picture is the central image. Remember the example from Chapter 7 in which the central image was a portable computer. The next step is to ask questions, adding the answers to the central image until you have a completed brain picture on your internal video screen. Never settle for less than the complete picture.

Customers generally fall into two categories. The first group is people who have a specific mental image of what they want. These customers, like the man who wanted a portable computer, will be able to describe their brain pictures to you. The second group of customers have only a vague idea of what they want. That doesn't mean they won't buy. It means that it is your job to turn their fuzzy ideas into clear images.

With both groups of customers, your goal is to move them as quickly as possible to a specific brain picture. The best way to do this is by asking them detective questions – questions that help both you and your customer define their brain picture.

General detective questions

The detective questions you ask can be either general or specific. Salespeople use general detective questions to begin a sales presentation or to start the sales conversation. This is a critical stage of the sale, because you need to build trust and rapport before you establish the customer's specific needs.

The following are examples of general detective questions:

- 'Have you bought from us before?'
- 'Have you used this type of equipment before?'
- 'Did you have anything special in mind?'
- 'Have you seen our new range?'
- 'Have you heard of our national distribution system?'
- 'Have you looked through our catalogue?'

Make eye contact and be friendly as you start a conversation along these lines.

Specific detective questions

Once you have begun a sales conversation you can establish the customer's specific needs. You want to understand or develop a clear shared internal brain picture with your customer.

Examples of detective questions to discover a customer's specific needs are:

- 'What colours do you prefer?'
- 'Do you have an actual delivery date in mind?'
- 'Do you have the specification details with you?'
- 'On what date can we inspect the site?'
- 'Can you call your office and find out what you are using now?'
- 'Is this for a formal or informal occasion?'

The next two Skill Builders will help you understand how these two types of questions can be used in a sale.

Skill Builder 59: hot fudge

As you read this sales conversation, which takes place between a waiter and customer in a restaurant, build up your own brain picture.

Waiter: 'What would you like for dessert?' (general detective question)
Customer: 'I'd like some fruit, please.' (general need)

Waiter: 'What type of fruit would you like?' (specific detective question)
Customer: 'Do you have any bananas?' (specific need)
Waiter: 'We certainly do. Would you like some vanilla ice cream with it?' (specific detective question)
Customer: 'That sounds nice.'
Waiter: 'One scoop or two?' (specific detective question)
Customer: 'Make it two.' (specific need)
Waiter: 'With hot chocolate or fudge topping?' (specific detective question)
Customer: 'Fudge, please.' (specific need)
Waiter: 'Would you like almonds, walnuts, whipped cream or chocolate chips on top?' (specific detective question)
Customer: 'Walnuts, please.' (specific need)

In this example, the waiter started off with a vague brain picture of 'a fruit'. By asking a specific detective question, 'what type of fruit?', he got the response 'bananas'. Immediately, the brain picture crystallized into one of a banana. From this point on, the waiter was able to build on that need by suggesting other items.

Are you able to picture a banana, with two scoops of vanilla ice cream and hot fudge sauce and walnuts? Of course you are. The waiter created a brain picture of a delicious dessert in the customer's mind and satisfied him by producing it.

Detective training

John and Shirley Ross own two Hallmark Gift stores in Atlanta that make impressive sales gains year after year and are regarded as models among the chain's 1500 North American stores.

Skill Builder 60: gift wrap and pink bows

Shirley Ross has mastered the selling of cards and gift wrap. She knows the way to stand, listen, smile, use detective questions and suggest items in *the last four feet*. As you read this sales conversation between Shirley and her customer build the brain picture in more and more detail.

A customer is looking down the aisles of cards as Shirley approaches.
Shirley (smiling): 'Good morning!'
Customer: 'Morning.'
Shirley: 'Looking for anything special?' (general detective question)
Customer: ' Looking for a 40th birthday card.'
Shirley: 'They're over here. Follow me.' (She takes the customer to the specific cards, and continues the conversation.) 'This is the big one. I know – I've been through it myself.' (Both laugh.) 'Is this for someone special?' (specific detective question)
Customer: 'Well, it's for my wife.'
Shirley: 'Let me see …' (She picks a few different themes and hands cards to the customer.) 'This is a funny one, this is a romantic one, this is very different.' (Shirley waits silently as the customer reads cards.)
Customer (laughing at the funny one): 'This is great!'
Shirley: 'Yes, I like that myself. Is it to go with a gift?' (specific detective question)
Customer (indicating a box under his arms):'A pair of running weights. She's going through a fitness phase. Not very romantic, I'm afraid.'
Shirley (smiling): 'Oh, I don't know … suppose I wrap it with some romantic gift wrap?' (specific detective question)
Customer: 'Would you do that?'
Shirley: 'Of course, let's go and choose something special.' (She walks to the gift wrap selection, helps the customer pick gift wrap and a pink bow and then wraps the gift while continuing the conversation.)

How did you do? Shirley Ross never leaves the customer while he's in her store. She listens, suggests, puts the cards in the customer's hands, discovers his or her needs by means of detective questions, and builds the sale. The add-on sale of the gift wrap and pink bow costs more than the card, but the customer is happy because Shirley has provided a quality service experience. It worked for Shirley Ross and it will work for you.

Skill Builder 61: self-check

Check your understanding of general and specific needs with this Skill Builder.

Below is a list of 10 customer statements. Read each one and decide whether the statement conveys a general or specific need. Test your answers first by constructing the type of brain picture suggested by each statement. A statement of general need will give you a fuzzy picture while a specific need will suggest a detailed one.

GENERAL   SPECIFIC

1. 'We want an alarm system that works.'
2. 'I need an air ticket to Oslo for next Wednesday morning.'
3. 'Have you got the software, Claris Works 2.0?'
4. 'We are working on the idea of re-tooling the division.'
5. 'Do you have a meat meal that's under 250 calories?'
6. 'It's in the budget, but that's as far as we've got.'
7. 'I want a life insurance policy but, at age 59, am I too old?'
8. 'What are the popular holiday resorts this year?'
9. 'We want some help with our tax return – it's due in next week.'
10. 'Do you have any Cummings recondi-tioned tractor engines?'

Suggested answers

General needs: statements 1, 4, 6, 8.
Specific needs: statements 2, 3, 5, 7, 9, 10.

The statements of general needs give a fuzzy picture:

1. 'We want an alarm system that works.'
4. 'We are working on the idea of retooling the division.'
6. 'It's in the budget, but that's as far as we've got.'
8. 'What are the popular holiday resorts this year?'

The statements of specific needs give clear mental pictures:

2. 'I need an air ticket to Oslo for next Wednesday morning.'
3. 'Have you got the software, Claris Works 2.0?'
5. 'Do you have a meat meal that's under 250 calories?'
7. 'I want a life insurance policy but, at age 59, am I too old?'
9. 'We want some help with our tax return – it's due in next week.'
10. 'Do you have any Cummings reconditioned tractor engines?'

Clarification

Customers also ask questions during the sales conversation in *the last four feet*. Sometimes the questions appear to be objections, but they are really clarifications of the customer's own brain picture or attempts to redirect you into offering the correct product or service. Whether consciously or not, customers are also trying to develop a clear mental picture of their actual needs. This is why they may appear to be hesitant or reluctant to make decisions.

The following Skill Builder helps to develop a clearer picture of the customer's needs.

Skill Builder 62: rosy gates

A salesperson is entering a customer's home to discuss a home security system. Read the entire sales conversation first.

Salesperson: 'Mrs Campbell! Good morning, I'm Mike Kremer from World Wide Security.'
Customer: 'Oh yes, you're on time, come in.'

Salesperson: 'Thank you. You certainly have a beautiful garden – those roses look like competition winners!'

Customer (laughing): 'Thanks, I've some of my white roses here in the living room.'

Salesperson: 'Oh, I must smell these … (smells) Mmm – lovely!'

Customer: 'Do sit down.'

Salesperson (seated): 'Thanks, Mrs Campbell. Well, you sent in our reply-paid postcard, detailing features of our security products that you were interested in.'

Customer: 'That's right – I took it out of the *Readers Digest*.'

Salesperson: 'That's a good magazine, isn't it? My wife has read it for years. (chuckles) She gets a really good laugh from those jokes.'

Customer: 'Yes, they are funny. Have you installed many security systems in this area, Mr … Mr …?'

Salesperson: 'Mike Kremer. Yes, over 20 homes on this estate have our system, Mrs Campbell.'

Customer: 'Really?'

Salesperson: 'Yes they do. Of course, for security reasons we don't give names and addresses of local clients, but I certainly can provide the names and phone numbers of clients in other cities' (takes out a list from briefcase and hands it over).

Customer (studying list): 'Hmm.'

Salesperson: 'You mentioned on your response card that you are interested in security gates?'

Customer: 'Yes, that's right. I do have an excellent alarm system in the house, but my company does not install gates.'

Salesperson: 'What system do you have now, Mrs Campbell?'

Customer: 'Well, our windows are wired with "Panic Alert".'

Salesperson: 'Oh yes, we know them well – an excellent company. In fact you can have your security gates armed through their system so you won't have two numbers to call if the need arises nor will you have two maintenance bills to pay.'

Customer: 'Really? How does that work?'

Salesperson: 'Well, because Panic Alert don't supply security gates we have a working relationship with them so that we can go through their systems.'

Customer: 'That's good to know.'

Salesperson: 'What types of gates did you have in mind?'

Customer: 'Well I'm not sure ….'

Salesperson: 'Well, for instance, do you want gates that are strictly functional or gates that are secure but elegant enough to complement your beautiful garden?'

Customer: 'I certainly want them to blend in with my house decor. It's just so shocking that we have to live our lives all locked in like this.'
Salesperson: 'Yes it is unfortunate. But better safe than sorry, eh? Let me show you some designs from our catalogue (takes out catalogue). This section here gives you some ideas on designs. Did you want gates for the front only?'
Customer: 'I only have a front gate, but I wanted my front door secured as well.'
Salesperson: 'Then let me suggest our Hazel Duo, here on page 77. What do you think?'
Customer: 'Hmmm.'
Salesperson: 'I think what's really nice about these are the flowers designs – they blend into a garden theme. You'll notice that there's space between the designs to open the front door with a key. Also they can be sprayed in the colour of your choice. What would yours be?'
Customer: 'I do like these, but are they secure?'
Salesperson: 'Mrs Campbell, when you close these gates, and run your hands over these locks I can guarantee you'll feel secure. Imagine going to bed at night safe in the knowledge that nothing could possibly harm you. Odd sounds in the night won't disturb you when you have World Wide Security looking after you.'

Let's stop here so that you can go back and analyse the sales conversation. Read the conversation again and, this time, analyse it using the Sales Mind Matrix in Figure 8.1 overleaf, and specific and general questions and needs.

Our suggested analyses are detailed below. We use italics to depict the Sales Mind Matrix and general and specific questions and needs.

Salesperson: 'Mrs Campbell! Good morning, I'm Mike Kremer from World Wide Security.' *Salesperson uses logic in approach.*
Customer: 'Oh yes, you're on time, come in.'
Salesperson: 'Thank you. You certainly have a beautiful garden – those roses look like competition winners!' *Salesperson uses picture, imagination and colour.*
Customer (laughing): 'Thanks, I've some of my white roses here in the living room.'
Salesperson: 'Oh, I must smell these ... (smells) Mmm – lovely!' *Salesperson uses smell.*
Customer: 'Do sit down.'
Salesperson (seated): 'Thanks, Mrs Campbell. Well, you sent in our

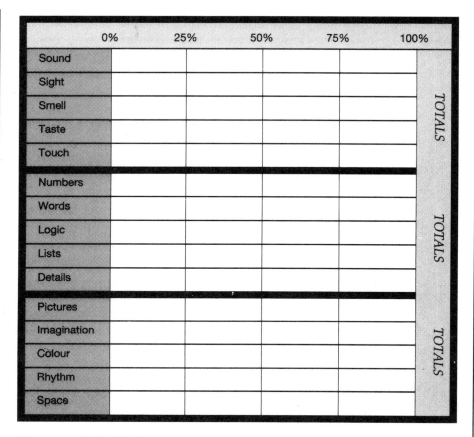

Figure 8.1   Sales Mind Matrix – complete

Salesperson's general questions:

Customer's general needs:

Salesperson's specific questions:

Customer's specific needs:

reply-paid postcard, detailing features of our security products that you were interested in.' *Salesperson uses details and lists. Refers to customer's general need.*

Customer: 'That's right – I took it out of the *Readers Digest*.'

Salesperson: 'That's a good magazine, isn't it? My wife has read it for years. (chuckles) She gets a really good laugh from those jokes.'

Customer: 'Yes, they are funny. Have you installed many security systems in this area, Mr … Mr …?' *Customer expresses a general need.*

Salesperson: 'Mike Kremer. Yes, over 20 homes on this estate have our system, Mrs Campbell.' *Salesperson uses numbers, logic and details.*

Customer: 'Really?'

Salesperson: 'Yes they do. Of course, for security reasons we don't give names and addresses of local clients, but I certainly can provide the names and phone numbers of clients in other cities' (takes out a list from briefcase and hands it over). *Salesperson uses numbers, logic and details.*

Customer (studying list): 'Hmm.'

Salesperson: 'You mentioned on your response card that you are interested in security gates?' *Salesperson asks a general detective question.*

Customer: 'Yes, that's right. I do have an excellent alarm system in the house, but my company does not install gates.' *Customer expresses specific need for gates.*

Salesperson: 'What system do you have now, Mrs Campbell?' *Salesperson asks specific detective question.*

Customer: 'Well, our windows are wired with "Panic Alert".'

Salesperson: 'Oh yes, we know them well – an excellent company. In fact you can have your security gates armed through their system so you won't have two numbers to call if the need arises nor will you have two maintenance bills to pay.' *Salesperson uses numbers and logic.*

Customer: 'Really? How does that work?'

Salesperson: 'Well, because Panic Alert don't supply security gates we have a working relationship with them so that we can go through their systems.' *Salesperson uses logic.*

Customer: 'That's good to know.'

Salesperson: 'What types of gates did you have in mind?' *Salesperson asks a general question.*

Customer: 'Well I'm not sure ….'

Salesperson: 'Well, for instance, do you want gates that are strictly functional or gates that are secure but elegant enough to complement your beautiful garden?' *Salesperson asks a specific question.*

Customer: 'I certainly want them to blend in with my house decor. It's just so shocking that we have to live our lives all locked in like this.' *Customer expresses specific need.*

Salesperson: 'Yes it is unfortunate. But better safe than sorry, eh? Let me show you some designs from our catalogue (takes out catalogue). This section here gives you some ideas on designs. Did you want gates for the front only?' *Salesperson uses pictures and asks a specific question.*

Customer: 'I only have a front gate, but I wanted my front door secured as well.' *Customer expresses a specific need.*

Salesperson: 'Then let me suggest our Hazel Duo, here on page 77. What do you think?' *Salesperson uses pictures, numbers, imagination and asks a specific question.*

Customer: 'Hmmm.'

Salesperson: 'I think what's really nice about these are the flowers designs – they blend into a garden theme. You'll notice that there's space between the designs to open the front door with a key. Also they can be sprayed in the colour of your choice. What would yours be?' *Salesperson uses numbers, logic, details, colour, space and asks a specific question.*

Customer: 'I do like these, but are they secure?' *Customer expresses a specific need.*

Salesperson: 'Mrs Campbell, when you close these gates, and run your hands over these locks I can guarantee you'll feel secure. Imagine going to bed at night safe in the knowledge that nothing could possibly harm you. Odd sounds in the night won't disturb you when you have World Wide Security looking after you.' *Salesperson uses logic, pictures, imagination, rhythm, touch, sound, sight.*

How do your analyses compare to the above?

Hint: Start tape-recording your sales conversations and role plays to analyse them as a fast way to incorporate the Sales Mind Matrix and detective questions into your everyday sales behaviour.

The complete picture method

The second method in determining the customers' mental pictures is using what we term the 'complete picture method'.

Clues

An effective detective observes his customers' behaviour from the moment they enter his line of vision. In Part Two, Chapter 6, 'Insight', we mentioned that more than half of the sales presentation is determined by your posture, gestures and eye contact. Well, the same could be said about customers' communication with you. What are their body posture, gestures and eye contact telling you? You need to become a keen observer of all your customers' behaviours.

Which products are your customers attracted to? What do they handle? What catalogues are they holding? Of which products and services do they have experience? What are they examining? Trying on? Trying out? Customers' behaviours will give you a good deal of information or clues about their brain pictures, so that you can start developing a mutual picture.

Observation

Next, you need to use all your other mental tools to find the missing pieces of the picture. By observing your customer's appearance you could get some excellent clues about the types of product or services they expect. Grooming gives you many clues – for example, immaculate hair, freshly polished nails and the wearing of expensive perfumes (sniff that one out!).

Shoes are a good clue; many sales detectives immediately examine the state of their customers' shoes to determine their customers' status. Are they clean and gleaming, or neglected? Expensive watches, diamond rings and necklaces are all-important clues about your customer's quality expectation and price range.

Where does the customer live? Residential address can give a good idea of income and status, as can the car they drive, or the clubs they belong to. Where do they go for their holidays – do they take costly trips around the world in Concorde or take camping holidays?

What books and magazines do they read? Consumer reports or trendy *Cosmopolitan*? If it's a consumer report, you know the customer is well armed with information and is looking for the right deal. In their office what do they have on their walls or on their shelves? Diplomas? If so, from when and from what dates? Do they display sports trophies or evidence of other hobbies? All of these are conversational pieces. Is their desk neat or messy? Are there pictures of their family, children, pets, cars or boats? A good detective is always looking for clues!

How do customers behave? Do they want to handle the item, examine it, read all the instructions or do they ask for your advice? Do they want to try it on? Get it working? Or do they want it assembled? These are significant clues about their expectations.

Completed picture

One of the benefits of listening and observing in pictures is that, if there are gaps in your brain pictures, it's simple to complete them. All you have to do is ask the right detective questions. Remember the waiter and the customer who wanted fruit for dessert? That brain picture was not detailed enough. Knowing that there was a gap, the waiter added to the picture of the banana, with two scoops of vanilla ice cream, walnuts and hot fudge!

There is no end to the interest and fun you can have being a sales detective. Remember to keep adding all the answers, all the clues, to the mental picture you are building up on your internal video screen of your customers' needs.

Keep adding to your brain pictures until you have *a completed picture*. No matter what you are selling, the complete picture method *works*.

Skill Builder 63: powers of observation

This skill builder will help your powers of observing customers' behaviour.

Irrespective of the products or services you are selling, take a trip, in the next few days, to a shopping centre and visit different types of stores. Observe the types of customers in each store. How are they dressed? What jewellery, if any, are they wearing? Look at their shoes. As a sales detective, what clues can you find? Observe how the customers handle the products. Notice exactly what they do, how they do it and when they do it. You will be surprised at the details you will observe. When you have practised this on 40–50 shopping customers, you will be well on your way to becoming an expert sales detective!

Review

To become a high sales producer, establish an accurate clear brain picture of the customer's needs. To do this, listen in pictures and then create a central image.

By asking detective questions you can build up a detailed brain picture of your customer's needs. Make certain that your picture is complete and shared with your customer.

Become a super-sleuth, a sales detective – be on the look-out for clues, they are everywhere to be found, especially in this book!

Skill Builder 64: sales detective review

On a separate piece of blank paper, Mind Map Chapter 8, 'Sales Detective'. You may look back.

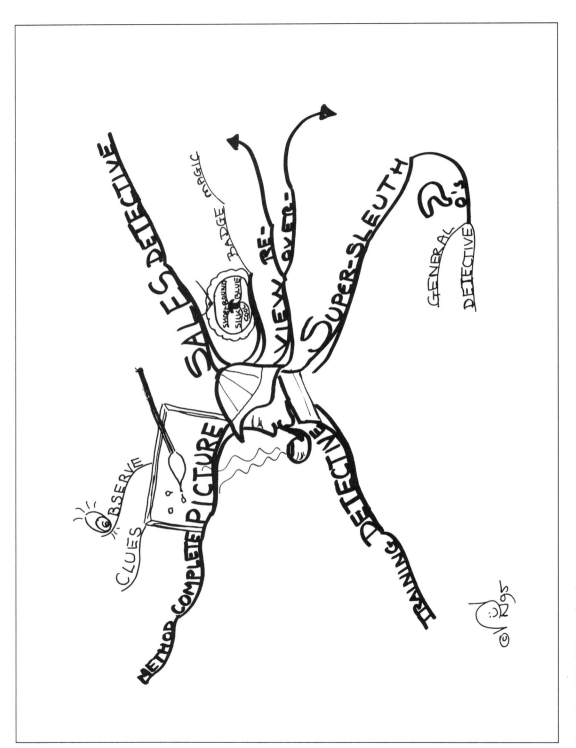

Figure 8.2 Mind Map: sales detective

9 Sales Compass

Give customers what THEY want

Your special monitor

Imagine you have been appointed to head the board of the largest and most successful company in the world. All the newspapers are speculating about your success and ability to run this giant corporation. On the first day in your new position, you meet your team of 20 executives who report to you and run the company. At 10 a.m. you call the meeting in the board-room. Everyone arrives on time, curious to observe you in action.

To a hushed audience, some sceptical, others appearing very superior, you stand and start to talk. You have done your homework by preparing with the help of a *special brain compass* that covers all the mental thinking skills, so nothing is left to chance. You used the special compass to organize your speech, to self-check it for accuracy, to organize your thoughts and present yourself at your best. Even more remarkable is the way this special compass helps you deliver your speech, for the design ensures that you cover each one of the possible thinking styles in that room.

During your talk the scepticism changes to interest, to wonder, and to excitement. You see people's faces light up, their backs straighten as their eyes are riveted on you. Every word you say is absorbed, every gesture you make sweeps the room in silent awe. You finish the presentation. The silence is broken with applause – thunderous applause – followed by a standing ovation. You are a sensation; you have sold them on you, you are a hit, a *star*!

163

As you walk out of the boardroom, you smile and think about your special brain Sales Compass that brought you stardom.

That very same compass, is here, in the following pages of *Brain Sell*, ready to make you a superior sales performer.

Overview

Once you have an accurate picture of your customer's needs, simply match these pictures and you will satisfy your customer. This can be done by developing an extension to the Sales Mind Matrix – the Sales Compass, the ultimate sale tool. Revealed here for the first time, the Sales Compass will act as both check and guide to ensure that you are using your Sales Mind Matrix correctly. Taken a step further, the Sales Compass allows you to analyse any conversation to determine the different mental skills your customer is using, resulting in a 'super match' – a gratified customer and a successful salesperson.

Match brain pictures

Retail selling is known for its short-cycle sales, where the purchase is often made in one presentation. A customer walks into a store with a certain result in mind. Some customers might be merely browsing for fun or looking around to see the new styles and colours. Others have a specific purpose – buying a new dress for an important party, getting a gift for a friend or picking up a pair of shoes for work. As the customer shops her mental video camera will be scanning the product, looking at window displays and display racks while talking to her friends and listening to the salesperson. Your aim is to become a mirror, reflecting back her mental image with your product and sales presentation.

In selling a service you have to work extra hard, as most services, such as insurance policies, financial services, advertising and mutual fund shares, are intangible. In many of these cases you have to create the picture of what the service does for the customer.

Selling large industrial products or selling to committees is more of a challenge. In a long-cycle sale, where more than one sales presentation is required, the customer's pictures of your presentation are altered or dimmed over time. So you need continually to reinforce the pictures, with follow-up letters, mailings, phone calls and additional sales presentations.

You continually have to match and build brain pictures in your customers' minds that lead to a satisfactory match of their needs with your product or service. When you build that picture in words, you should accentuate the customer's preferred senses and mental thinking skills. You will be able to do this with help from your Sales Compass. We started to demonstrate the Sales Compass in the previous chapter with the 'Rosy Gates' Skill Builder 62 (page 153).

Be flexible

In 1979 David Rapaport was the top producer at Levitz Furniture's Golden Glade store in Miami, enjoying sales of more than $1 million a year, and the commission that went with it. Richard observed his skills while designing a selling skills programme for the company.

In 1990 Richard returned to ask David what had changed in the last 11 years. 'I'm still the top producer' David said, 'but the customers have changed. Why, we now have people in the store from throughout the world – from India, the Middle East, the Caribbean, Russia, you name it, and they are in here buying furniture.'

Asked what was the secret of selling to such a diverse group of customers, David replied, 'You have to be more flexible. You have to think like they do, meet them in their own space.'

David was right. He had found his Sales Compass and was successfully using it!

Skill Builder 65: go shopping

Go shopping for an item you would like to buy. During the sales conversation ask yourself whether the salesperson is effectively using salesenses and mental skills:

- sound?
- sight?
- smell?
- taste?
- touch?
- numbers?
- words?
- logic?
- lists?
- details?
- pictures?

- imagination?
- colour?
- rhythm?
- space?

Upon completion of this Skill Builder you should be aware of what makes a good sales presentation and what makes a dull one. More importantly, you are learning what you need to do to make your sales presentations sparkle.

Skill Builder 66: great speakers

Consider some of the great sales speakers: Winston Churchill; Martin Luther King; John F. Kennedy; Adolf Hitler; Nikita Khrushchev; or Muhammed Ali. You can now do a quick check of these speakers by asking the following questions:
Did these speakers uses **salesenses** in these speeches? Tick off your answers.

- Did they make good use of their voice?   Yes_____   No_____
- Did they make a strong visual appeal?   Yes_____   No_____
- Did they use sensory words and images?   Yes_____   No_____
- Did you feel any emotion?   Yes_____   No_____

Did these speakers use the following **mental skills** in their speeches? Tick off your answers.

- numbers?   Yes_____   No_____
- words?   Yes_____   No_____
- logic?   Yes_____   No_____
- details?   Yes_____   No_____
- lists?   Yes_____   No_____
- pictures?   Yes_____   No_____
- imagination?   Yes_____   No_____
- colour?   Yes_____   No_____
- rhythm?   Yes_____   No_____
- space?   Yes_____   No_____

What is a great speaker but a great salesperson? He sells ideas. His brain pictures match and become your brain pictures! That is why people will listen for hours on end – because the entire range of their mental skills are being appealed to! Every single brain in the audience will react to these speeches.

Whole-brain intelligence

In Chapter 1, we mentioned Dr Robert Ornstein's research on the brain. During this work he found that when different mental skills are stimulated you achieve a powerful result. In maths, we know that one plus one equals two. However, Ornstein found that when one side of the brain was 'added' to the other side, the result was often five to ten times more effective! This information is crucial in sales. The more you use salesenses and the ten different mental skills in your sales, the more creative you will be.

One of the best

While Richard was designing a sales training programme for Mayors Jewelers in the mid-1980s, he worked with one of their best salespeople Michael O'Mahony. Michael emigrated to the United States in 1974 with $500 in his pocket and joined Mayors as a salesman.

Michael's selling skill became a legend not only at Mayors but right across the country. What made Michael so great? Well, Michael used more of his brain than most salesperson. He would use his salesenses, inviting his customers to sit down, have coffee or a glass of wine, and talk to them about … themselves! Being a great sales detective, he would find out their birthdays and anniversaries and send them cards.

He used more of his ten mental skills than most. In one case a South American client wanted a certain item of jewellery that was only available in another store. Unfortunately the customer was about to go to the airport and fly home, so could not wait for the transfer of the item to Michael's store. The creative Michael drove to the other Mayors store, collected the item and drove onto the airport only to find that the plane was ready to take off. Undeterred, he got permission to board the plane, found his client seated, with safety belt on, and made the sale! Today Michael is chief executive officer of a successful art retail chain for Fidelity Investments of Boston.

More of their brains

In our studies of high-producing salespeople around the world – from John Deere in Germany, to Norman Ross in Australia, to Macys in the USA, to the Wool Board in South Africa, to Selfridges in the UK – we found an interesting correlation. Not only were their sales consistently higher than the average – often 200–300 per cent higher – but, when we interviewed them, we found that what distinguished these people was that they were using all their mental skills and were selling with their whole creative brain!

Ornstein's findings have special importance to those of us educated in the West, where we have been trained in the three Rs – reading, writing and arithmetic – all left cortical subjects. It is hardly surprising that most of the sales training materials produced in recent years has been 'left cortex' dominant!

We have traditionally considered people who are artistically talented, musical, sporty, good with their hands and a bit 'dreamy' to be poor academic material, not really the right material to make a success in the professional world. All evidence now suggests that this is only part of the picture, and that the successful 'creative' or 'artistic' person is also using their whole-brain skills, just the same as the academic person.

The first conclusion to be drawn from Ornstein's work is that everyone is both potentially scientific and artistic. If we are more 'right cortical skills' dominant or more 'left cortical skills' dominant it is not because of inherent disability, but simply because one side of our brain has had more opportunity to develop than the other. This means that you need to develop your whole Sales Mind Matrix, all the ten mental skills and your salesenses. If you were playing tennis and had a strong right arm, you would need to strengthen your left arm to have a perfectly balanced body. The same applies with your Sales Mind Matrix; you must use all your mental skills and salesenses to maximize its potential.

Application

The second conclusion is that customers have a preferred mental skill, or skills, which they use when communicating with you. If the customer's preferred mental skill is 'logic' you can expect her to ask you logical questions or describe her needs in a logical way. For example:

Customer: 'How does this fit together?'
or
Customer: 'I want a computer that is easy for my kids to use. One that has a step-by-step approach.'

If the customer's preferred mental skill is 'imagination', however, you might hear the following:

Customer: 'I can think of a whole lot of applications for this foodmixer not

mentioned in the instruction book!'
or
Customer: 'I want to take an exotic holiday, something very unusual.'

A customer might use one, two or more of her mental skills in the conversation. Your task is to identify which mental skill or skills she is using and then tune your Compass to match it with your responses. Once you have matched it, you can strengthen your sales conversation by including more mental skill elements.

| **Discover, match and build a stronger picture in your customer's mind.** |

Let's examine how this would work with the previous examples:

Customer: 'How does this fit together?'
Salesperson: 'It's quite simple. You see, all the parts are numbered A, B, C and they all fit together in order. You'll find it fun to use and it's built to last.'
or
Customer: 'I want a computer that is easy for my kids to use. One that has a step-by-step approach.'
Salesperson: 'This computer has on-screen, easy-to-follow, colour-coded instructions that were designed by kids for kids! It's both easy and fun to use and it has a freephone number so you can call in for free expert help!'
or
Customer: ' I can think of a whole lot of applications for this foodmixer not mentioned in the instruction book!'
Salesperson: 'That's great! You should send those ideas to the manufacturer. Who knows, you might get a great gift! Meanwhile, you'll be making all those mouthwatering recipes for your family and friends.'
or
Customer: 'I want to take an exotic holiday, something very unusual.'
Salesperson: 'How about a canoe trip into the hidden rivers of Fiji?'

Could you see how the salesperson was able to match the customers by using his Sales Compass?

The Sales Compass

The Sales Compass is designed to help you understand your customers, your own use of your salesenses and the ten mental thinking skills. Think of your brain as a compass: instead of North, South, East and West, you have a device as pictured in Figure 9.1. Each time the customer uses one or more of the 15 mental skills depicted, your mental Sales Compass automatically points to it.

For example, when the customer says, 'How many colours does this come in?', your mental Sales Compass, flashes 'COLOUR' on your internal video screen, denoting that the customer is currently using their 'colour' mental skill. Now you can match it with both words ('Why, we have three colours – blue, green and orange') and actions ('Let me show you all three').

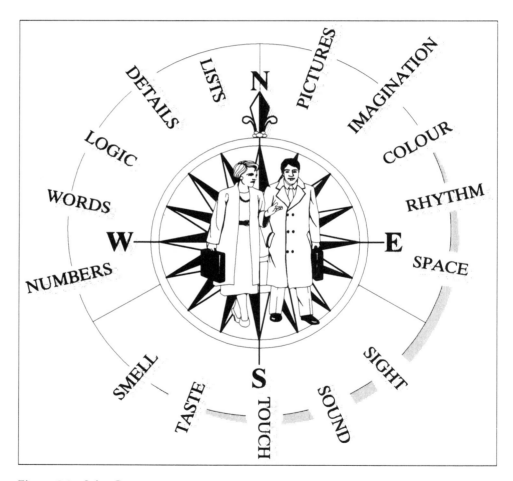

Figure 9.1   Sales Compass

The Sales Compass is the most effective way of completing the customers' brain pictures. It is a mental checklist which covers your customers' multisensory information and ten mental skills, all from your Sales Mind Matrix.

By using the Sales Compass, you will have 100 per cent accuracy on how to match your customers' pictures.

All their mental skills

If the customer is using logic and imagination, the super salesperson matches the logic and imagination mental skills. He might also mention other senses and mental skills, because people use all of these, and each can be activated in a sales presentation.

Questions to be asked when using the Sales Compass are:

- 'What mental skills has my customer covered?'
- 'Have I matched my customer's main interest, senses and mental skills?'
- 'Can I add any additional senses and mental skills to the sales conversation?'

Skill Builder 67: a puzzle

As you read the sales conversation below, use the Sales Compass matching chart in Figure 9.2 to check the progress of the sale.

A sales conversation is taking place in *the last four feet* between a customer and salesperson. The customer is looking for an educational toy as a gift, and the salesperson is suggesting a jigsaw puzzle.

Customer: 'Well, I don't know what's the value of a jigsaw puzzle!'
Salesperson: 'When you say "value", do you mean educational or money value?'
Customer: 'To me, jigsaws were really hard to do. I used to get frustrated with them. I could never find the right pieces. Somehow I remember I only got a few colours to match and could never get the whole picture completed.'
Salesperson: 'So you feel that jigsaw puzzles were difficult?'
Customer: 'Maybe they weren't so much difficult as I didn't know how to do them. Have they made them any easier?'
Salesperson (pointing to the back of the box): 'Well, there are instructions, written in easy-to-understand language and made simple to follow. See, here are a series of steps to follow. First, you place all the pieces on a flat surface. Next, you see if there are any of the same colours to group. Then you start with the four outside corners and work inwards.'

	CUSTOMER COVERED: YES NO	SALESPERSON MATCHED: YES NO	SALESPERSON ADDED: YES NO
SENSORY DATA			
Sound			
Sight			
Smell			
Taste			
Touch			
MENTAL SKILLS			
Numbers			
Words			
Logic			
Lists			
Details			
Pictures			
Imagination			
Colour			
Rhythm			
Space			

Figure 9.2 Sales Compass matching chart

Customer: 'That makes a lot of sense. I wish they'd done that years ago (laughs), it would have made them a lot easier. Let's see, there are some attractive ones here. What a lovely picture! I love the colours of those flowers on the hills. How many pieces in this puzzle?'

Salesperson: 'This has 2000, and takes about 14 hours to complete. It really is pretty, isn't it?'

Customer: 'Do you think kids get any educational value from these?'

Salesperson: 'They most certainly do. A jigsaw puzzle is a really good way for a child to develop mental skills.'

Customer: 'What do you mean?'

Salesperson: 'The puzzle challenges their imagination in finding the right pieces and their logic in fitting the pieces together. There's analysis skills working from the sides to the centre. Their colour co-ordination skills and sense of rhythm of how the pieces flow are developed. It also helps them to create.'

Customer: 'To create, how's that?'

Salesperson: 'They see the whole picture on the box and they start to build from one piece at a time. This calls for perseverance and feedback. Sometimes the pieces fit, sometimes they don't, so they learn to keep trying till their jigsaw matches the picture on the box. Isn't that how we create in real life – through trials with feedback and perseverance?'

Customer (after a pause): 'I suppose you're right. I'll take it – it's a wonderful gift.'
Salesperson: 'Would you like it gift wrapped? We have some beautiful gift wrap paper.'

How did you do? Below is our suggested analysis of how the salesperson applied the Sales Compass. By carefully listening to the customer, the salesperson could establish the customer's key mental processes, build up a brain picture on the customer's needs and then match it with the appropriate sales language and product. Let's go back over the sales conversation to see how the Sales Compass is applied.

Customer: 'Well, I don't know what's the value of a jigsaw puzzle!'
Salesperson: 'When you say "value", do you mean educational or money value?'
Customer: 'To me, jigsaws were really hard to do. I used to get frustrated with them. I could never find the right pieces. Somehow I remember I only got a few colours to match and could never get the whole picture completed.'

Using the Sales Compass the salesperson establishes that the customer had problems with logic and details in the past and then confirms this, with the next detective question.

Salesperson: 'So you feel that jigsaw puzzles were difficult?'
Customer: 'Maybe they weren't so much difficult as I didn't know how to do them. Have they made them any easier?'
Salesperson (pointing to the back of the box): 'Well, there are instructions, written in easy-to-understand language and made simple to follow. See, here are a series of steps to follow. First, you place all the pieces on a flat surface. Next, you see if there are any of the same colours to group. You then start with the four outside corners and work inwards.'

Salesperson completes the customer's brain picture by stressing, the instructions, in easy-to-understand words, pictures, details, colour and logic.

Customer: 'That makes a lot of sense. I wish they'd done that years ago (laughs), it would have made them a lot easier. Let's see, there are some attractive ones here. What a lovely picture! I love the colours of those flowers on the hills. How many pieces in this puzzle?'

Customer confirms that her brain picture is completed by asking a question on NUMBERS ('How many pieces in this puzzle?') which the salesperson, using the Sales Compass, answers in the next sentence, adding LOGIC, PICTURE, COLOUR, and NUMBER.

Salesperson: 'This has 2000, and takes about 14 hours to complete. It really is pretty, isn't it?'
Customer: 'Do you think kids get any educational value from these?'
Salesperson: 'They most certainly do. A jigsaw puzzle is a really good way for a child to develop mental skills.'
Customer: 'What do you mean?'
Salesperson: 'The puzzle challenges their imagination in finding the right pieces and their logic in fitting the pieces together. There's analysis skills working from the sides to the centre. Their colour co-ordination skills and sense of rhythm of how the pieces flow are developed. It also helps them to create.'
Customer: 'To create, how's that?'
Salesperson: 'They see the whole picture on the box and they start to build from one piece at a time. This calls for perseverance and feed-back. Sometimes the pieces fit, sometimes they don't, so they learn to keep trying till their jigsaw matches the picture on the box. Isn't that how we create in real life – through trials with feedback and perseverance?'
Customer (after a pause): 'I suppose you're right. I'll take it – it's a wonderful gift.'
Salesperson: 'Would you like it gift wrapped? We have some beautiful gift wrap paper.'

The salesperson with the help of the Sales Compass has used WORDS, DETAILS, PICTURES, IMAGINATION, LOGIC, COLOUR and RHYTHM in his sales presentation to achieve this result. The customer finally confirms that her Brain Picture has been completed.

A key skill

Your ability to listen and observe while using the Sales Compass to build up a customer's brain picture is a key mental skill to develop. Being able to match a customer's brain picture in your sales presentation will prove invaluable in satisfying your customer.

Practise listening to conversations – any conversations – to develop your awareness of how people are using their specific mental skills. This will advance your use of the Sales Compass and your skill to build brain pictures.

Start matching

Once you have a detailed brain picture with all the specific mental skills, start matching. You are probably doing this now! If a customer were to ask you the price, which is a number on the Sales Compass, you respond by giving the price. Now you are aware of the wide range of mental skills your customer is using, you can match your customer to his satisfaction. The Sales Compass is a tool for understanding and matching those mental skills that the customer is using. The brain picture is a way of remembering and building on that information.

Auto pilot

As you work with your Compass you will find that it becomes second nature to use it in all sales conversations. Be aware of what mental skills your customer is using by having your mental Compass in your mind. Each time you hear a different mental skill used, swing your mental pointer to match and simply tick it off. This way you will have a mental check of which skills have been used and which ones have not. Remember when you first learnt to drive a car? You were so conscious of all the things you had to do. Start the engine, release the brake, look in the mirror and on and on. Once you had been driving for a few months, it all became automatic. Nowadays you can drive the car away, listen to the radio and hold a conversation simultaneously! Yet some part of your mind is still checking – checking the instrument panel, checking your speed, looking for police cars and dangerous situations ahead. You will develop the same skill with your Sales Compass. Part of your mind will be checking off what mental skills the customer has used and then automatically incorporating them into your conversation and checking also what mental skills the customer has not used and also building those into your conversation, ensuring that your customer enjoys a rich, full picture of the product or service you are selling.

Skill Builder 68: dinner party

Read the following conversation between the customer and sales-person. Each time the customer mentions a mental skill or the salesperson matches or adds to it, tick it on the Sales Compass matching chart in Figure 9.3.

A customer and salesperson are in *the last four feet*, discussing catering services.

Salesperson: 'How many people are you expecting, Mrs Taylor?'

Customer: 'Oh, about 60. You know, the numbers are always changing. The last party I catered for 50 and 70 came. I'm not bothered about the numbers. You can cater for 80 to be on the safe side.

Salesperson: 'Did you have any particular menu in mind?'

Customer: 'Well, first let me tell you about the theme, then maybe you can recommend a menu. This year I'm having a New Orleans party. Guests will come dressed appropriately, I'm having a jazz band and tons of champagne. My party planner, Jean Dorkins – quite the best you know – is using her imagination to turn my house into a typical New Orleans home.'

Salesperson: 'How interesting! Will you expect my staff to dress accordingly? We do have the proper outfits for a slight extra charge, Mrs Taylor.'

Customer: 'Well, of course they must, Henry. I want the evening to be a night everyone will remember forever. My parties always are, you know. Make certain that everything matches the theme.'

Salesperson: 'Like a continuous jazz beat, with matching colours, wines, foods and centrepieces. That should give everyone a great feeling with the music ringing in their ears for days ... .'

Customer: 'Exactly, I do enjoy using your services, Henry – you really understand me. Get the best centrepieces you can – flowers if possible. Red roses might be the answer, dozens of them.'

Salesperson: 'That's just what I was thinking. The colours will be wonderful and oh, the fragrance! It will be the talk of the town.'

Customer: 'Now, how can we have the menus printed so that guests will want to take them home as souvenirs?'

Salesperson: 'I have an artist who can give us a few suggestions. We can use a special paper that has a rich texture – your guests won't want to put them down.'

	CUSTOMER COVERED: YES NO	SALESPERSON MATCHED: YES NO	SALESPERSON ADDED: YES NO
SENSORY DATA			
Sound			
Sight			
Smell			
Taste			
Touch			
MENTAL SKILLS			
Numbers			
Words			
Logic			
Lists			
Details			
Pictures			
Imagination			
Colour			
Rhythm			
Space			

Figure 9.3   Sales Compass matching chart

Skill Builder 69: computer express

Read the following conversation between the customer and salesperson. Each time the customer mentions a mental skill or the salesperson matches or adds to it, tick it on the Sales Compass matching chart in Figure 9.4.

Customer: 'Can you help me please?'

Salesperson: 'Certainly, what did you have in mind?'

Customer: 'I'm setting up a home office and I need a computer.'

Salesperson: 'Great, you've come to the right place – "Computer Express". My name is June McGovern.'

Customer: 'Jeff Lewin.'

Salesperson: 'Nice to meet you Jeff (shakes hands). Now tell me what you need. You said you are setting up a home office, right?'

Customer: 'Yes, I'm branching out on my own, so I'll need to make my office as functional as possible.'

Salesperson: 'What type of work do you do, Jeff?'

Customer: 'I'm a schoolteacher, but now I'm selling health insurance.'

Salesperson: 'Sounds like me. I graduated in fine arts and here I am selling computers!'

Customer (laughs): 'Yes, it's certainly a crazy world!'

Salesperson: 'Have you used a computer before?'

Customer: 'Well, my brother has a Macintosh which we play games on.'

Salesperson: 'Can you type?'

Customer: 'Yes, I can.'

Salesperson: 'Well you're going to type letters, write proposals and keep a set of accounts, right? I can see you hitting that keyboard in no time!'

Customer: 'I suppose so.'

Salesperson: 'You are going to need to produce a quality image if you're working from home. That way you'll give the impression and confidence of being a well established company.'

Customer: 'Yes, that's right.'

Salesperson: 'I suggest that you invest in a laser printer. It gives work the appearance, feel and tone of quality, especially if you print on good paper.'

Customer: 'Good idea, I'll certainly need that.'

Salesperson: 'Do you already have a customer base?'

Customer: 'No, I'm starting from scratch.'

Salesperson: 'Any idea of the numbers you'll have in the first few years, Jeff?'

Customer: 'Hopefully, a few thousand.'

Salesperson: 'Then you are going to need about 100 MB, hard drive.'

Customer: 'If you say so. What does 100 MB mean?'

Salesperson: 'It's the storage capacity. 100 MB will be ample for the first few years, giving you plenty of room for what you're doing. Do you have a fax machine?'

Customer: 'No, that's on my list of purchases.'

Salesperson: 'Well you can get a fax/modem built in, saving you money in extra equipment and it gets you into the information highway. You'd quickly be up to speed. I can hear you buzzing away on it now!'

Customer: 'How about software?'

Salesperson: 'I recommend a straightforward integrated program – it gives you powerful tools to run the business with.'

Customer: 'Integrated ... sounds interesting – what's it actually mean?'

Salesperson: 'It's software that's all in one – a word processor with spell checker and thesaurus, spreadsheet with charting and a data base. How's that sound?'

Customer: 'Hmm … but what's this all going to cost?'

Salesperson: 'Jeff, there's a wide range of prices from … to … . Now we have a clear picture of your needs let's move to the computers and give you some hands-on experience.'

Customer: 'I'm already getting a feel for this.'

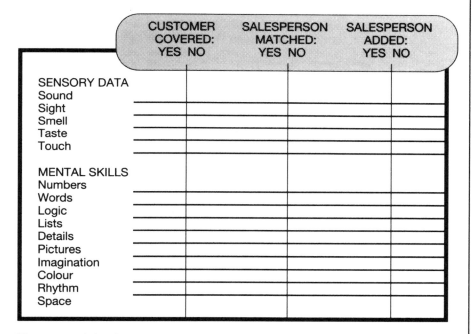

Figure 9.4   Sales Compass matching chart

Selling services

The Sales Compass works for services as well as products. Services are often intangible items, where you need to create a picture in the customers' mind and then gain some type of commitment or action.

Take fundraising as an example, regarded as an intangible sale and rather difficult (asking the public for money!). As the fundraising industry grows, more and more fund raisers are using telephone selling as their main thrust.

Fund raisers

Selling over the phone has been reduced to reading a prepared script and working on a percentage of the contributions collected. Had a solicitation lately? Did you hear the script being read? Did you have a chance to ask questions? Could the caller answer your questions? By now you will have gathered that prepared scripts, no matter how well written, make very limited use of the Mind Sales Matrix!

Let's listen into a phone conversation. Here the caller (salesperson) is calling ex-pupils of the Prince Edward Grammar School. The school solicits donations from their ex-pupils from time to time.

Salesperson: 'Dr Edwards, my name is Martin Blain, calling you on behalf of Prince Edward Grammar. As you know, a few years ago you were generous enough to give us £150, and we wondered if you would kindly consider increasing your donation this year?'
Dr Edwards: 'Who did you say you were?'
Salesperson: 'Martin Blain.'
Dr Edwards: 'From where?'
Salesperson: (pause) 'I'm calling on behalf of Prince Edward Grammar, your old school.'
Dr Edwards: 'Martin, this is a bad time to call me.'
Salesperson: 'We just wanted to know if we could count on you donating, say, £300 to our school's building fund.'
Dr Edwards: 'What are you building now?'
Salesperson: (long pause) 'Well, since the government cutbacks we don't have sufficient funds for our buildings.'
Dr Edwards: 'What buildings?'

Let's try that again, this time without a script and using our Sales Compass and the complete picture method.

Salesperson: 'Dr Edwards, this is Martin Blain, I'm a student at Prince Edward Grammar, your old school. How are you?'
Dr Edwards: 'I'm fine, Martin, but I'm a bit rushed right now. What do you want?'
Salesperson: 'Dr Edwards if you are in a hurry, I'll call back. I thought it was only us A-Level students who had no time, but I imagine being in Medicine you know all about that too?'
Dr Edwards: 'Somewhat.'
Salesperson: 'When did you leave Prince Edward Grammar, Dr Edwards?'
Dr Edwards: '1978.'
Salesperson: 'Weren't you in the school cricket team that year?'
Dr Edwards: 'Why, yes, how did you know?'
Salesperson: 'We've just published a sports book with photos of each year's

cricket and soccer team since 1965. I remember seeing your name.'
Dr Edwards: 'Really? What a wonderful idea.'
Salesperson: 'Would you like me to send you a copy?'
Dr Edwards: 'Would you?'
Salesperson: 'Of course. Is your address still 27 Grovesland Road, Southgate?'
Dr Edwards: 'Yes. When do you think I'll get it?'
Salesperson: 'Right away. My reason for calling is about our building fund for our new gym.'
Dr Edwards: 'What was wrong with the old one?'
Salesperson: 'You saw it back in 1978. Since then the school has doubled in size and government funding has been drastically cut back. Could we count on you for a few hundred pounds, and I'll put the confirmation in with the sports book?' (pause)
Dr Edwards: 'Put me down for two hundred.'
Salesperson: 'Thanks so much, Dr Edwards. I'll post the book right away. I know you'll enjoy it immensely.'

Skill Builder 70: Dr Edwards

How did Martin Blain do in his second conversation with Dr Edwards? Using the Sales Compass matching chart in Figure 9.5 analyse the conversation

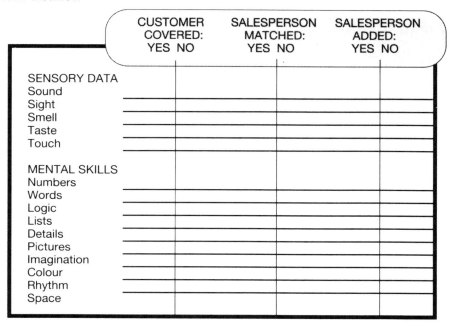

Figure 9.5   Sales Compass matching chart

Review

It's time to review. We have come a long way together and covered a lot of new ground. Selling is communication: the stronger your communication abilities the better results you will enjoy in all aspects of your life. Communication is one brain connecting with another: the stronger that connection the better the result.

When you meet someone you love – a child, a relative, a friend – do you hug them with one arm, or do you put both your arms around them and squeeze them and make the strongest connection you can? It's the same with brain-to-brain communication. You need to make the strongest connection you can, wrapping your whole brains around each other.

In Part Three, we have taken you on a journey in which you have explored your own and your customer's brain. Chapter 7 covered the mind search, in which you discovered your mental video screen. This was followed by Chapter 8, 'Sales Detective' and the development of super-sleuth skills, with detective questions and observation. Lastly, in Chapter 9 you were introduced to the Sales Compass – a mental compass that allows you to match your Sales Mind Matrix with that of your customer and yourself.

These skills have one common goal, to help you make a strong connection so that you and your customer share the same pictures – pictures you can match with your products and services. As you use and master these skills, you will communicate better, sell better and live better.

Skill Builder 71: Sales Compass review

On a separate piece of blank paper, Mind Map Chapter 9, 'Sales Compass'. You may look back.

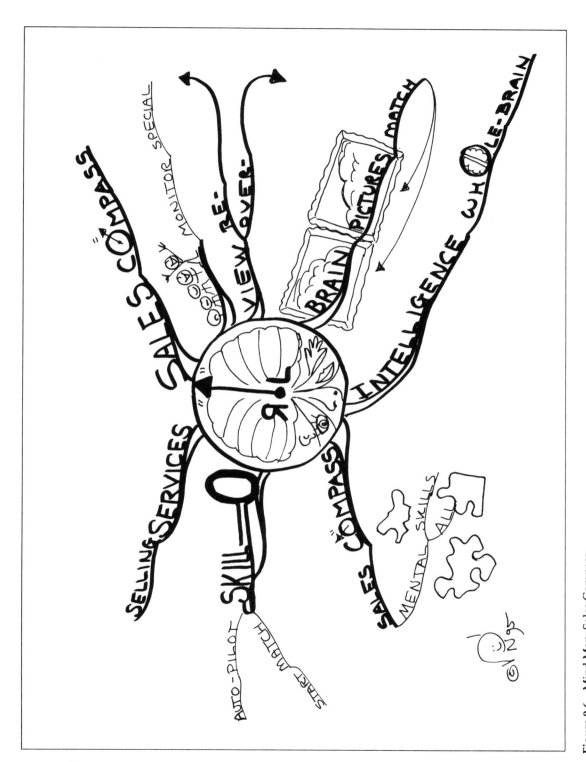

Figure 9.6 Mind Map: Sales Compass

183

PART FOUR

SuperSellf

Introduction

Brain Sell is a series of whole-brain selling skills. In the first three Parts we covered numerous new sales skills, all building up to Part Four.

In Part One, we introduced you to an in-depth understanding of the miraculous brain. The first chapter, 'Whole-brain Selling' dealt with the ten different mental skills of your whole creative brain, and emphasized that the customer's brain is 'truth-seeking', needing the correct information to make the right decisions. Chapter 2 showed how information enters your brain through your senses and how it can be communicated back to your customers' five senses for maximum sales effect. Chapter 3, 'Memory Imprints', explained how to remember customers' names and faces. With two simple techniques you learned how to make a lasting mental impression of all and on all your customers.

Having understood how to use your Sales Mind Matrix, together with your magnificent memory, Part Two showed how to become an information expert and emphasized the importance of the mind–body connection in selling. Chapter 4, 'Infocentre', gave you the keys to mastering information in this 'information age'. You are 'an information centre' able to answer any question on your product or service and satisfy your customers. Chapter 5, 'Mind Maps', introduced a new whole-brain technique which enables you to absorb and retain large amounts of information quickly. Chapter 6, 'Insight' dealt with the mind–body connection, explaining how these two parts must work in harmony for superior sales performance.

This chapter revealed how to get both your mind and body in perfect shape.

Now that you had successfully mastered the information your customers require and were developing both a healthy mind and body, the aim of Part Three was to master the sales conversation and the interaction with the customer. Chapter 7, 'Mind Search', revealed how to use your internal video screen to study customers' brain pictures. Developing the foundation skill of using your internal video screen is core training in *Brain Sell* technology. Chapter 8, 'Sales Detective', showed how, with the aid of sales detective questions and other super-sleuth skills, you can enter your customers' minds and reproduce their brain pictures! This new mental skill helps you to *accurately* discover and clarify your customer's real needs.

Chapter 9, 'Sales Compass', explained how to achieve a satisfied customer. This means giving your customer whatever she wishes. To do this you simply match exactly what your customer wants with information and products or services, using the Sales Compass. The Sales Compass allows you to analyse a conversation to find out the different Sales Mind Matrix skills your customer is using. You begin to understand sales conversations in a totally new light. This results in satisfied customers who will come back to you again and again.

Brain Sell, Part Four, 'SuperSellf' comprises three further chapters. Chapter 10 explains how to program your thinking to achieve the outcomes you want. The next chapter describes how to structure your sales conversation for the maximum sales impact. The final chapter explains how to live at your best and enjoy endless abundance. Let's examine each chapter in more detail.

Chapter 10 is called 'Sales Focus, Create the Outcomes you Desire'. By understanding how your thinking and perceptions condition your sales behaviour in *the last four feet* (the distance between you and the customer), you will soon change the way you view customers. You will learn secrets to improve your sales and improve your powers of observation. This chapter introduces the insightful 'aim frame', a technique to help you stop making excuses and to point you in the right direction.

Chapter 11, 'Power Hooks, the Secret to Memorable Sales Presentations', gives you five key hooks to incorporate into your sales conversation. Each power hook acts as a mini-connection in your customer's mind, ensuring that what you say is long remembered and acted upon. You will be able to use these power hooks in all future sales conversations. As a result, more people will remember what you say, quote you, think about you and consider you an expert!

Chapter 12 is entitled 'SuperSellf. Experience SuperSellf and Unlimited Prosperity'. All your life you have been 'selling yourself'. SuperSellf takes you into the different roles and circumstances of daily life and explains how to use *Brain Sell* sales technology to be at your best. If you are making a speech, talking to your bank manager, socializing at a party or presenting your ideas at a meeting you are 'selling yourself'. For each of these different situations, go back to the specific Skill Builders and techniques in Parts One, Two and Three for review and mastery.

By introducing your whole creative brain into the sales process, you will unleash a new force in your life. *Brain Sell* technology leads to whole-brain creative thinking, and your perspective and behaviour will change in many pleasant ways. When you have mastered *Brain Sell*, you will be well on your way to achieving higher sales. You will enjoy your work with less stress while building a base of loyal customers who will keep returning to you.

Part Four will show how you can:

- set and reach outcomes you desire;
- redirect your thinking;
- increase your powers of observation;
- be master of your thoughts and behaviours;
- make memorable sales presentations;
- discover your SuperSellf;
- live life to its full potential.

Once again, this Part contains Skill Builders that are all designed to help you sell better. As we suggested in Parts One to Three, to make the best use of this book, first skim through it very rapidly to get a general understanding. Then read it in depth and do all the Skill Builders in the proper sequence. For maximum benefit we recommend that you spend a week on each chapter, giving yourself time for in-depth reading, study, practice-time for the Skill Builders and time for your brain to absorb and integrate all the new material into your everyday sales behaviours.

When you have finished the in-depth reading, keep the book with you for daily reference. Record all your thoughts, new ideas and new techniques.

Use the sales management section, found in Appendix A, as your personal development programme. And, finally, please write to us telling us your successes, stories and copies of sales graphs at the address found in Appendix B 'The Brain Seller's Network'.

10 Sales focus

Create the outcomes you desire

Pre-thought

Imagine you wake up one morning in the year 2995, and you are the same age as you are now. You sit up in bed and think back over the last thousand years. You think about the evolution of man and how, over those years, he developed a sixth sense – the sense of pre-thought. This has been a useful addition to your mental skills. With pre-thought, you can think about what you want, and then it happens. For instance, if you want a friend to phone you, you pre-think it and then your friend calls. It has certainly made your sales job easier. You must pre-think the results you want and they happen. Life has become so much more enjoyable!

Well, you don't have to wait a thousand years, because the future is here. Through understanding how to use your amazing brain, you can enjoy pre-thought. This chapter tells you how to use your thinking as a new force, just like this pre-thought.

Overview

By understanding how your thinking and perception condition your sales behaviour in *the last four feet*, you will create the outcomes you desire. You will learn two skills: to rehearse the sale mentally; and to improve your powers of observation. This chapter details the insightful 'aim frame', a technique to help you stop making excuses and to get you to the right destination. Once again, your Sales Mind Matrix is being developed to maximize your sales ability.

Two powerful secrets

Mental rehearsal leads to sales success

Jack Teichman was a bulldog of a salesman. At 200 pounds, 6 foot 2 inches with a thick Middle-Eastern accent, Jack would attach himself to each of his customers to discover their needs in detail.

In the late 1970s, while acting as a consultant to Sol Polk, president of the well-established, highly successful Polk Brothers chain of appliance and furniture stores in Chicago, Richard was lucky enough to study Jack's sales techniques. To this day, Jack is regarded as one of the all-time great salesmen. He earned more than $100 000 in 1978 alone, working only nine months, and taking luxury vacations with his wife to exotic places such as Italy and Greece.

When customers walked into Jack's department, he approached each one and simply stayed with them. Jack followed customers around as they strolled through the washers and dryers, the refrigerators, dishwashers and air conditioners, watching and listening to everything they did and said. If the customer ignored him, Jack would step back a little to give them 'space'. Some customers, who knew what they wanted, might buy a washer in 10 minutes. Other customers might take an hour or more to choose a certain model. Jack didn't care about the time – he stayed nearby and made himself available.

When his customer asked a question Jack would always be an 'Info-centre' (for more details, refer again to Chapter 4), having already taken the time to read the instruction manuals for the items he sold. 'I'm an expert' he would say, 'Ask me any question about what I'm selling and I've got the answer.'

Over lunch one day, Richard asked Jack why he was so successful. Jack pondered the question for a moment and replied, 'In my thoughts, I picture every customer as satisfied. I've already met their needs in my mind before I even say "hello". Then, I just stay with them, listening and match-ing their needs.'

Jack had found two powerful secrets about using his Sales Focus skill that few salespeople understand:

1. You start the sale with the result of a satisfied customer in mind.
2. You make every sale twice – first in your mind, then in real life.

As you go about your work, do you visualize the desired result, as Jack does? Or do you sometimes say to yourself, 'There's no way I'm going to make this sale' or 'What time is lunch?'

Start with the result

Let's start you on the road to success with Jack's first secret: starting the sale with the image of a satisfied customer in your mind. It might surprise you to know that most salespeople take little control over their thinking as regards what result they want. They will make appointments, spend hours travelling, have samples and price lists ready; yet with all this preparation they will have spent little or no time thinking through the result they want.

In a long-cycle sale, where you might need to make three or four presentations to a committee – where decisions are not made instantly –

Figure 10.1   Start with the result

you need to think through the stages of the sale. The first meeting might be to simply collect information. Here, the desired result of the first call might be to collect quality and detailed information.

Skill Builder 72: pre-thinking

On a separate sheet of paper create a Mind Map with an image of a future event in the centre. Construct branches of events you are pre-thinking or planning prior to the main event – for example, a special holiday or an anniversary party.

Why is it so important to start with the result? Our brain tends to look for patterns and completion. For example, if you heard 'Mary had a little … .', you might add the word 'lamb', because your brain tends to complete things. Unless you have a result in mind, you randomly choose anything. When you are aiming for a result, your salesenses search for the clues to help you attain it and reach completion. So knowing the result you want to achieve is an important first step.

Lost sales opportunities

The *Wall Street Journal*, in its Centennial Survey, stated that 25 per cent of American shoppers complain about poor service, citing instances, for example, of when salespeople are on the phone and ignoring the customer. We have read similar reports regarding European shoppers. Imagine how many sales could be made if the salespeople had been aiming to please the customer.

While sales can be lost for many reasons, there is only one reason for a sales success – the customer is satisfied! As a salesperson whose income depends on satisfying customers your Sales Focus plays a key part in satisfying the customer in every sale.

In 55 years of combined sales consulting, Tony and Richard have talked to salespeople of all types. Whenever we asked a salesperson 'Why didn't you make the sale?', the answer would often be something like 'I just knew this customer wasn't going to buy'. When asked how he knew this, the salesperson would say 'Well, I just had this feeling about it.'

How can you decide if your customer will buy on the basis of your feelings? Feelings are constantly changing. Your feelings may change if the temperature in the room is too hot or too cold. They may change if you had two cups of coffee for lunch or if you're expecting a call from your friend tonight. Thousands of fleeting thoughts affect your feelings daily and make them bad decision-makers.

Another standard reply of unsuccessful salespeople is 'I just couldn't picture the customer buying this item – it was too costly for her.' When asked how they knew that, the answer again is often 'Well, I didn't know – I just imagined it.'

Consumed with the result

Frances Pinter owns a UK book publishing company. She has succeeded in a male-dominated world, starting from scratch in 1973, with no publishing experience, against everyone's advice and with only £750. Today she runs a successful and profitable multimillion-pound company and is one of the leading publishing figures in the world. As chairperson of the Independent Publishers Guild, she hosted publishing delegations to Japan, Korea, Poland and China.

Frances told us how she managed to get through those difficult start-up years when she had no knowledge of the business, nor any contacts to help her. 'I would imagine what I wanted to achieve. I was always very positive; there was no consideration of failure. I would not allow negative thoughts to dwell in my mind. All day, every moment of the day, I was consumed with the result, as though I was looking down a tunnel and I knew when I got to the end, I would have made it.' Frances had learned how to make Sales Focus work for her: she knew the result she wanted!

The prejudgement trap

It's an easy trap to think that you know what's happening in your customer's head, but your thinking can frequently lead you astray and cause you to prejudge situations incorrectly. The customer may be feeling happy or angry or bored or any of a dozen other emotions when you walk into her office. You can imagine many things about that customer, but you won't know for sure unless you talk to her and study her body language. And the more you talk to her and observe her, the more you will learn and the better your chance of satisfying her needs.

What we have learned from Jack Teichman and Frances Pinter is that you must make your thoughts work *for* you, by visualizing the results you truly want. Irrespective of what you are selling, if you don't know where you are heading, your thoughts will lead you anywhere, so always have the result in mind.

Make every sale twice

Jack Teichman's second secret is that you must make every sale twice – first in your mind, then in the real world. That means that you can rehearse mentally the way you want the sale to happen. You can change the result simply by your thought process. Here's how.

Aim frame

One of our associates, Lucy D. Freedman, is an expert in communication skills. She has an excellent technique, the 'aim frame' which helps you focus your attention on satisfying your customer.

The aim frame is a four-question mental checklist that you run through before every sale to keep you targeted:

1.   What result do I want to achieve?
2.   How will I achieve this result?
3.   What are the probabilities of achieving this result?
4.   What have I previously learned that will help me achieve my result?

A salesperson like Jack knows exactly what he wants to achieve – pleasing the customer – and he aims for that goal with each one. When problems arise, he recalls what he has learned earlier and tries different techniques to achieve his aim. Even a top salesperson like Jack knows he won't always be successful, but he doesn't let that get him down. He just keeps his aim in mind when he talks to the next customer.

Reframe

Lucy found that people also needed to *reframe* when things did not turn out as planned. They should ask themselves these four reframe questions:

1.   What is the situation?
2.   Why did this situation arise?
3.   What factors caused this situation?
4.   What needs to be done?

These two sets of questions will keep you on track during the day as you deal with customer after customer.

A new view

Now, taking a lesson from Jack Teichman, as you plan your next presentation, sales call, or approach your next customer, ask yourself the aim
frame questions.

Q. What result do I want to achieve?
A. A satisfied customer.
Q. How will I achieve this result?
A. By thinking of the results I want and doing whatever is necessary
    to satisfy the customer.
Q. What are the probabilities of achieving this result?
A. We have a comprehensive choice of products using the latest tech-
    nology, at competitive prices. I know that, by spending time and con-
    centrating on my customer's needs, I will satisfy my customer and
    make the sale.
Q. What have I previously learned that will help me achieve my result?
A. I should stay with my customer to help her choose the right product,
    even if this means transferring the product from another branch, mak-
    ing follow-up telephone calls, or putting in a special ordering from
    the factory. I will satisfy the customer's needs because I have the skills
    and knowledge to do so.

You can now approach the customer with your 'Aim Frame' mind-set!

Mental check

Keep yourself in the aim frame and use the four questions detailed above
as a continuous mental check to keep you aiming in the right direction –
to please the customer. Now that you know the aim frame, every time you
meet a new customer you should rehearse mentally the four questions,
which we repeat below:

1. What result do I want to achieve?
2. How will I achieve this result?
3. What are the probabilities of achieving this result?
4. What have I previously learned that will help me achieve my result?

When needing added guidance to achieve the desired result ask yourself
the four reframe questions:

1. What is the situation?
2. Why did this situation arise?
3. What factors caused this situation?
4. What needs to be done?

These questions work equally well for customers! Imagine you have an angry customer who has a complaint about a product or service recently purchased from you. You ask him the four reframe questions:

1. What is the problem (regarding this product/service)?
2. Why did this problem arise?
3. What factors caused this problem?
4. What needs to be done to rectify this problem?

The customer will soon be on your side once you have helped reframe his dissatisfaction. All you did was change the word 'situation' to 'problem'!

Skill Builder 73: a recent visit

Think of a customer – one who you will visit in the next few days. Name that customer and the product or service that will be of interest in the space below. Next answer the aim frame and reframe questions that follow.

Customer name _____ **Product/service** _____

Aim questions

1. What result do I want to achieve?

2. How will I achieve this result?

3. What are the probabilities of achieving this result?

4. What have I learned previously that will help me achieve my result?

Reframe questions

5. What is the situation?

6. Why did this situation arise?

7. What factors caused this situation?

8. What needs to be done?

Another view

As previously mentioned, a customer can use his aim frame too. This is an interesting thought and could certainly assist you in thinking through your sales presentation from another angle.

Imagine you are a sales consultant about to make a sales presentation to a client on a new range. You have given this presentation a good deal of thought and preparation. As a final check, you change places, placing yourself in your client's shoes and asking yourself the client's aim frame questions (be careful, however, to base your answers on what you *know* about the client and not what you *imagine*).

1. What result do I (the client) want to achieve?
2. How will I (the client) achieve this result?
3. What are the probabilities of achieving this result?
4. What have I (the client) previously learned (in my dealings with this company) that will help me achieve my result?

Let's now step back into the sales consultant's shoes. Knowing what is going through the client's mind as regards the above four questions, would you change your presentation in any way?

Using your video camera

Why is your mental aim so important? When you start with the result you tell your mind to start searching for the information you need to achieve that result. By having the result in mind you increase your powers of observation.

Have you ever seen a favourite film twice? When you saw it the second time, you probably noticed scenes that you didn't remember from the first time. That's because there was just too much to take in the first time. Maybe you were concentrating on the plot and missed some dialogue. Maybe you identified with the main character and ignored the soundtrack or the special effects. Although your brain absorbs all information immediately, what you hold in your *conscious* mind – that is, what you are currently thinking about or processing – all depends on your mental focus.

Think of your brain as a video camera with your eyes as the lenses and your ears as the microphone. You are the director, the photographer and the sound engineer making your own personal movie. Each second you are deciding where to aim your camera and what to record. You cannot understand everything, because there's just too much happening around you. You select what's of interest to you and aim your video camera in that direction.

Skill Builder 74: increase your powers of observation

This enjoyable and easy Skill Builder will improve your powers of observation. All master salespeople are great observers; they watch every move their customers make, their every facial expression and notice even whether the pupils in their eyes are expanding or contracting.

By improving your powers of observation you will be able to apply all the new skills we have covered to improve your sales.

Practise observation daily in different locations – at home, in the car, in a restaurant, in an office, going for a walk. Select a certain colour and see how many items you notice that contain that colour. Next, count how many different sounds you can hear while closing your eyes to cut out distractions. Notice the different sensations you experience. A sensation can be the feeling of air entering your nostrils as you breathe or the feeling of your clothes brushing against your skin.

A. Look around you for ten separate objects with red in them and list below.
    1.
    2.
    3.
    4.
    5.
    6.
    7.
    8.
    9.
    10.
B. Listen for five distinct sounds and list below.
    1.
    2.
    3.
    4.
    5.
C. Notice five different sensations you are presently experiencing and list below:
    1.
    2.
    3.
    4.
    5.

Just as you need to clean the lens on your video camera and service your microphone you need to improve your powers of observation to help complete your aim frame.

Review

Successful salespeople know how to use their Sales Focus by starting every sale with the image of the result they want to achieve. By using the aim frame questions they are able to achieve this result.

They know that every sale happens twice – first in your mind, then in *the last four feet* the actual sale. Learn to use the power of your Sales Focus to get what you want. To help in mentally rehearsing each sale, use the aim frame and reframe questions.

By using your Sales Focus, you are developing that amazing sixth sense. Your brain is working for every future sale; even while you are asleep you are working on strategies to reach the aim frame.

Skill Builder 75: sales focus review

On a separate piece of blank paper, Mind Map this chapter 'Sales Focus'. You may look back.

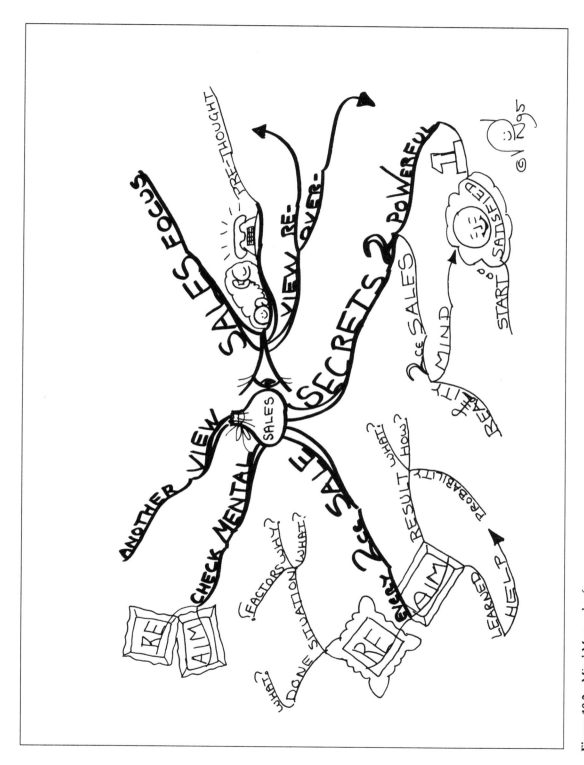

Figure 10.2 Mind Map: sales focus

11 Power hooks

Secrets to memorable sales presentations

The most successful salesperson of all time

Imagine meeting the most successful salesperson of all time! You excitedly wait for the great day to arrive. You dress in your best clothes, arrive at the meeting extra early with your tape recorder ready to capture every word.

Eventually, the moment comes. You are ushered into a beautiful room. The walls are lined with hundreds of books, the floor covered with a thick Persian carpet. At a huge oak desk sits the world's greatest salesperson. You swallow hard and miss a breath as you sit down next to this legendary figure. After shaking hands, you ask your one question about selling: 'How can I become famous like you?' The face smiles, and a voice replies, 'Make every one of your customers positively remember you forever.'

As you leave the room your mind is racing. 'If I could make every one of my customers positively remember me forever, then my customers would recommend me to their friends. Soon I'd have hundreds of customers. My sales would go through the roof, I would become famous … the question is, how do I do this?

The answer to that question is given in this chapter, for when you have finished it, you will have the new *Brain Sell* technology to make every one of your customers positively remember you forever. Read on!

Overview

Discover how to incorporate rhythms to make your sales conversation memorable. Each word power hook acts as a connector to your customer's mind, ensuring that what you say is long remembered and acted upon. You will be able to use these power hooks in conversations with friends, peers, and managers. The result will be more people remembering what you say, quoting you, thinking of you and considering you an expert!

The sales memory curve

This chapter outlines the amazing new discoveries about how your customer's brain, your own brain – all brains – remember. We will show you the main peaks of memory during any sales presentation or communication. Once you have learned how your memory works and what these high points are, we will convert them into power hooks that will allow you to ride the sales memory curve in every sales presentation and sales communication in the same way that an expert surfer rides the ocean waves. Many people surf, with identical surfboards and in identical ocean conditions, but the difference between the master and the disaster is that the master knows the rhythms and watches for them. The disaster tries to do the same – monitors the waves, picks a point – but, as it is the wrong one, gets slammed into the ocean bed! The difference is knowing the right rhythm so that you can act on the high point and ride it. The same applies to this chapter. The expert salesperson will know when to use the power hooks we will reveal, how to turn them to his advantage and how to get more satisfied customers.

The application of these hooks is a new revolutionary sales formula. They use verified psychological research on the rhythms of your brain's memory functions to allow you, the salesperson, to adjust your own sales presentation to take best advantage of these power hooks in *the last four feet*.

How could we forget you!

A middle-aged couple walked into the Wentworth Gallery in Boca Raton, Florida. After browsing through the paintings on display, they stopped in front of a $2 000 McNight silk-screen serigraph print. As they lingered there, David Holden went to work. He approached the couple, positioned himself in *the last four feet*, introduced himself and immediately launched into a power chat about the McNight print. He spoke rapidly and with authority on the artist's abilities and the unusual nature of the artwork.

With a few specific detective questions, Holden learned that they were looking for a piece of art for their study, how the study was decorated and the size of the blank wall. Moving back to the McNight print, Holden emphasized its exceptional characteristics with eloquent hand gestures. Then he handed them a measuring tape to see if the print would fit their study wall. It did.

Looking directly at the lady, Holden asked, 'Do you love it?' She nodded. In a commanding voice, just below a shout, Holden said 'Then buy it!' She did.

After the couple left, Richard came out of the manager's office where he had been observing and asked Holden if this powerful, emotional closing technique always worked for him.

'Not always,' he replied, 'but it worked this time because I could see from their body language, their gestures, their expressions and answers to my questions that they loved this piece and needed a nudge to make them decide. I guess that's what makes me the number one producer in the chain. And a high percentage of my customers return to buy from me again. They say, "how could we ever forget you!".'

Skill Builder 76: do customers remember you?

Do your customers remember you? And do you remember your customers? Here is a quick check to see how well you are doing. The following 'Yes/No' questions will give you an idea of how memorable you are. Record your answers as you go along.

		YES	NO
1.	Do you remember your customers' names and use them during the sales conversation?		
2.	Do your customers call and ask for you by name?		
3.	Do you remember what you say to each customer?		
4.	When you close, do you analyse what you did to make it happen?		
5.	Has a customer paid you a compliment in the last two days?		
6.	Do you find out your customer's personal interest and use it in your conversation?		
7.	When you feel the customer won't buy, do you analyse why?		
8.	Do you listen to the key words a customer uses and incorporate them into conversation?		

YES   NO

9.   Do you know of things you say that interest your customer?

10. Do you know how to involve your customer in the conversation?

11. Do you take Mind Map notes?

12. Do you use colour in your notes?

13. Do you have a favourite colour that you are known by (e.g. a red tie or scarf)?

14. Do you say something outstanding and memorable in every sales conversation?

15. Do you always start with a 'bang' and end with a 'bang'?

16. Do you practise associative techniques to remember your customers' names?

17. Do you think your memory is excellent?

18. Do you use memory techniques to remember product information?

19. Do you remember your key customers' birthdays and send them cards?

20. Can you recall the five most important sales you have ever made?

SCORE

If you scored 18 or more 'yeses' you are doing well.

Powerful presentations like Holden's don't happen by accident. They make use of the way your brain learns and remembers information. The following Skill Builder that will help you understand how your memory works.

Skill Builder 77: memory check

Below are 35 words. Read each word in order only once, down the page. Don't study them.

bargain
shoe
show
apple
child
monkey
book
mother
and
castle
of
studio
and
of
manual
fat
of
road
child
Elton John
rain
award
nature
of
monkey
and
winter
question
light
monkey
plant
and
knife
butter
rope

Cover the list over and write down all the words you can remember in order in the box overleaf.

Now, go back to the original list and circle the words you remembered.

Why did you remember those words and not others? Most people who do this Skill Builder are more likely to remember the *beginning* words (bargain, shoe, show) and the *end* words (knife, butter, rope) than the words in the middle. *Repeated* words (monkey, and, of) are remembered as are the distinctive words (Elton John) or any words with a *personal* association.

Five keys

Because your customer's memory works in the way demonstrated by the previous Skill Builder, we can formulate five keys to a memorable presentation:

1. Starstart – The beginning
2. 'Play it Again Sam' – What you repeat several times
3. Emphasize the unusual/outstanding
4. Over to you – What involves the customer
5. Grand finale – The close

Knowing that your customer's brain reacts in this way gives you the perfect formula: you can mirror your customer's brain to make a memorable presentation. You have the exact rhythm power hooks between the customer and salesperson and the salesperson and the customer.

Let's consider how to apply each of the five keys to a memorable sales presentation.

Key no. 1: starstart – the beginning

Your probable results in the previous Skill Builder demonstrated the necessity of a forceful introduction. That doesn't mean speaking in a loud, obnoxious voice. It means using your voice to convey your enthusiasm and energy to the customer. When you connect, your energy links with your customer and your customer's attitude and enthusiasm responds accordingly. Quite often, you'll find that your customer starts to speak a little louder, stands up straight and smiles more frequently.

Why do you have such an effect? Because personal enthusiasm is contagious. When you watch an exciting football, basketball or tennis match, you can really feel the enthusiasm start to rise in the crowd. The players' energy is being transferred back to the spectators. The same transfer of energy will happen with your customers. When you are really enthusiastic about your products and services your customer will sense this excitement too.

In long-cycle sales (where more than one sales presentation is required), you need to introduce yourself, by giving your name, smiling, making eye contact and, if possible, shaking hands: 'Good morning, I'm Shirley Petterson, how are you?' Asking the customer a question gets immediate involvement. In your next few sentences use some salesenses in your conversation (for more details on Salesenses refer back to Chapter 2):

'I read in the *Financial News* of your great annual results – must make you feel good to see those record breaking sales profits and hear all the compliments.' You have now placed a multisensory picture in your customer's mind – right in the beginning of the conversation!

In short-cycle sales (where usually only one sales presentation is required), you need to start a sales conversation and get immediate involvement. Although it's important to obtain the customer's name and use it, the challenge is how to make your opening different and therefore memorable. Compare, for example, the opening, 'Can I help you?' with 'Welcome to the greatest hardware store in the world! I'll bet you that we have exactly what you're looking for. Tell me what you need.'

In a setting, with repeat customers, especially if you know their names and their buying habits (see Chapter 3 for name-remembering techniques), you should mention your customer's name, and ask a general question to begin the sales conversation. For example, you might say, 'Hello Mrs Gordon, it's good to see you again. How's your beautiful daughter doing at school?'

You may use these approaches and adapt them to your style, or you could be creative and invent your own greetings. Your objective is to project your personality and to connect with your customer. Finding out the customer's name and introducing your own is an important start and adds the personal touch.

How would this apply to writing advertising copy? The first sentence becomes even more important now that you know the brain remembers those first few words. Look through a popular magazine and study the advertisements. Read the copy and decide whether the first sentence is memorable for each advertisement.

In what other applications is a memorable beginning important? A sales letter, opening a meeting, company presentations are just a few. Can you think of more?

Key no. 2: 'Play it again Sam' – what you repeat several times

In the skill building test you remembered the words that were repeated. Your customer is more likely to remember the hooks that you have repeated regularly in your presentation. But which hooks should you repeat? This is where you can use brain pictures. First, establish your customer's brain picture and his specific needs, then repeat those specific needs regularly. An average salesperson might handle a customer who is interested in buying a camera for his daughter, like this.

Salesperson: 'Now, as I understand it, you want this camera as a gift for your daughter.' (specific detective question)
Customer: 'That's right. It has to be automatic. She's not mechanically minded, so it has to be easy to use.' (specific need)
Salesperson: 'How much did you want to spend?' (specific detective question)
Customer: 'Around £120.' (specific need)
Salesperson: 'Right. Let me show you this Fuji DL-300. It's on sale for £95. It has excellent features for the money. For instance, it has a motorized winding that winds the film out of the cartridge first and then pulls it back in as you expose the frames. That way, if you accidentally open the back, you save your pictures.'
Customer: 'Hmm.'
Salesperson: 'It also has an ultrafast shutter speed which means that ... .'
Customer: 'Excuse me, but is it easy to use?' (specific detective question)
Salesperson: 'I'm coming to that ... .'
Customer: 'Let me think about it.'

Why did this sales conversation end so abruptly? The salesperson was paying so much attention to this product that he forgot about his customer's brain picture. Although the camera had many excellent features, the customer wanted to match his brain picture of his daughter with an easy-to-use camera. The result was disappointment for both the customer and the salesperson.

Let's replay that scene to see how repeating the customer's key needs can lead to a sale:

Salesperson: 'Now, as I understand it, you want this camera as a gift for your daughter.' (specific detective question)
Customer: 'That's right. It has to be automatic. She's not mechanically minded, so it has to be easy to use.' (specific need)
Salesperson: 'Easy to use. Okay. How much did you want to spend?' (specific detective question)
Customer: 'Around £120.' (specific need)
Salesperson: 'Right. Let me show you this Fuji DL-300. It's on sale for £95. It's the easiest-to-use camera we have in your price range. Because it's fully automatic all your daughter has to do is to place the film here (closes the back of the camera) and she's ready to shoot. It's that simple.'
Customer: 'Hmm.'
Salesperson: 'Can you see your daughter enjoying this? It's that simple to load. When she completes the role of film, she just pushes this lever and the film automatically rewinds. Then the back opens ready to unload the film.'

Customer: 'That's it?' (specific detective question)
Salesperson: 'That's it. It's all-automatic and simple to use. Let me recommend two rolls of the new Kodacolor Gold 100 film. Now, will that be cash or credit card?
Customer: 'Do you take the Master card?'
Salesperson: 'We certainly do.'
Customer: 'Well, make it two rolls then.'

What a difference! This time the salesperson was listening to the customer's specific need for an easy-to-use camera. He then created a brain picture for the customer and repeated the specific need four times. By regularly repeating the words 'automatic' and 'easy-to-use', the salesperson ensured that the customer would remember those all-important points.

Remember, when using your power hooks, to listen for your customer's needs and then to repeat those specific needs regularly, if possible using multisensory language as you repeat your points.

Key no. 3: emphasize the unusual/outstanding

In the Skill Builder you remembered the unusual words, such as Elton John, because your brain is constantly seeking unusual and fresh stimulation and entertainment. If you can present the key features and benefits of your product to your customer in a funny or unusual way, your power hooks will be imbedded into your customer's mind.

Think of the most memorable television commercials you've seen. In this situation, the advertiser only has 15, 30 or 60 seconds to get you to remember his products. On TV you'll see kitchen knives that cut through thick pieces of wood, detergents being mixed in a cocktail glass, car polish removing the stains left by a red-hot flame. These creative commercials are designed to appeal to the brain's imaginative capacity and to its predisposition to remember that which is outstanding or different from the norm.

To emphasize the unusual while using your power hooks, you need something appropriate to say. Even if your product or service seems to be totally dull it undoubtedly has some outstanding features or uses that make it unusual! While working with J. Lyons, Richard overheard the following conversation between two women shoppers and a liquid detergent salesperson in a London supermarket.

Salesperson (smiling): 'Excuse me ladies, I'm Lawrence Hopper, I wanted to ask you if you were the two ladies I had in my dream last night?'

Lady Number 1 (amused): 'What dream was that?'
Salesperson: 'The dream about meeting two rich, beautiful ladies, about your ages, who own their own yacht?'
Lady Number 2: 'Really!'
Salesperson: 'Yes, and it was floating in a sea of the most incredible detergent I ever saw – rich white foam with strong cleansing power.'
(Ladies Number 1 and 2 both laugh.)
Lady Number 1: 'How much is this?'
Salesperson: 'It's on introductory offer at 50 pence a carton. Would you like one each?'
Lady Number 2: 'Why not? Let's try it.'

In your power hooks, you can also use your voice to emphasize your point. You can gesture, tell colourful stories or give unusual demonstrations. The aim is to make your sales presentation different so that your customer will remember you.

Key no. 4: over to you – what involves the customer

Betty Day was in her late 50s when Richard worked with her at CAPS (Central African Pharmaceuticals) in Harare, Zimbabwe. Richard had designed a selling skills programme for Lancôme Cosmetics of France, and Betty and Richard were training Lancôme beauty consultants in department stores throughout Central Africa.

Betty's key strategy was to get the customer involved. Once she had established what her customer wanted, she would take out a sample of that product – a cleansing cream, lipstick or perfume – and start to apply it to her customer. Betty knew that, once her customer became involved with the Lancôme product, she could create a picture of beauty that the customer desired. The scents, the textures and the colours of her cosmetics all worked together to create a multisensory effective sales presentation. As a result, her power hooks would make their way almost effortlessly to the mutually desired outcome.

In the Skill Builder you remembered words with which you had associations and had personal connotations. Therefore, whatever your product or service, you should devise ways to involve your customer. Remember how David Holden encouraged his customers to measure the print to see if it would fit on their study wall? When you get your customers physically involved you are connecting with their Sales Mind Matrix (for more details see Chapters 1 and 2).

Have you noticed which salesperson has a crowd of people standing around their booth at an open air market? It is the one who is demonstrating his products or services, and who engages in a lively, colourful conversation with the crowd. If you're selling a mattress, get your customer to lie down on it. With a camera, let your customer hold it, focus it and shoot a few imaginary photos. If selling clothing, get your customer to try the garment on. If selling fast foods, have samples available. Keep thinking of ways to get your customer physically involved in your presentation. Keep making as many connections as you can. Connections activate your customers' Sales Mind Matrixes.

Key no. 5: grand finale – the close

Mystery writers, Hollywood film producers and top sales producers know the importance of saving the climax for the end. A powerful ending will bring the customer back for more. Think of *Jaws*, *Back to The Future*, *Star Trek* and *Rocky*. These blockbuster films had powerful climaxes – and a series of sequels. Think about the end of a symphony, how the music builds to a climax. Think of the end of the Olympic games with its grand finale, or the end of a great party, when the band plays the last dance and everyone joins in.

In the 35-word Skill Builder, did you remember the last few words: knife, butter, rope? Most people do. It therefore follows that if you give your customer a powerful end to your sales presentation you will be remembered long after the sale has been completed. For example, if the customer has just bought an item from you and is leaving, say 'You have made a wise decision and I know you will have years of enjoyment from this, Mr Wells. Come back and tell me about it.' How often have you heard those words when you made a purchase? Probably never. But think about those ending words: 'You have made a wise decision … you will have years of enjoyment … . Come back and tell me about it.' You have reinforced the buying decision. You have left the customer with a positive feeling about the purchase and have also used a power hook to embed the positive message in the customer's mind.

In a long-cycle sale – for example, when selling to an industrial client – you may end the sales conversation with 'I will contact you in five days to make certain our delivery was to your satisfaction'. You are reinforcing the buying decision, speaking with confidence and leaving a strong positive impression in your customer's mind.

Satisfaction guaranteed

In a short-cycle sale, sometimes a customer will leave your store without a purchase but will come back the next day to buy your product or service. For a customer who is undecided or who wants to check other competitors, your powerful ending can be the lure that brings her back.

Your power hooks can lead to one logical conclusion, that of asking a satisfied customer for the order. As simple as this sounds, thousands of unsuccessful salespeople forget this vital point every day. If you ask for the order and the answer is positive, you are both satisfied. If the customer is not ready, you should continue your power hooks and, when you think the time is right, ask again. There are two essential points to remember.

1. When you summarize always give your customer a choice of two items to consider, both of which will lead to a sale. Some typical choices are 'Cash or credit card?', 'Red or blue?', 'Wednesday or Thursday delivery?' and 'This model or that one?'. That little word 'or' carries a terrific impact when you use it to ask for the order.
2. Once you ask the decision question, stay silent. Your customer needs time to decide on a response. No matter how long it takes, wait for your customer's answer. By talking first you derail your customer's thought process and reduce your chances of a satisfied customer.

Memorable presentation

How can you put all your power hooks into action to create more sales for you in *the last four feet*? Here's a Skill Builder to help you remember the five important power hooks. The aim of this Skill Builder is to use the mental technology of Mind Mapping. With practice, using Mind Maps, you will be able to structure a powerful sales presentation for any product or service you are selling.

Skill Builder 78: power hooks

Choose a product or service that you enjoy selling. On a blank sheet of paper draw your Mind Map making the central image an item of your choice. Then add five branches to represent the five keys to a memorable sales presentation:

● Beginning – Starstart

- Repeat – 'Play it again Sam'
- Unusual/outstanding
- Involvement – 'Over to you'
- Close – Grand finale

Complete the five branches of your sales presentation Mind Map by adding your own power point comments about the item.

Review this Mind Map frequently adding any further ideas you may have or learn from your daily sales presentations. You could enlarge it and place it on a wall for daily reference.

Have you ever asked for an order only to find that the customer was not ready to buy? Here follows an explanation for this and advice on what to do when it happens.

The convincer

Bill Huckabee, an associate and brilliant consumer researcher, believes that every customer has a 'convincer' hidden somewhere in his brain. This is a mental mechanism that determines when your customer will buy. Convincers all have two important variables.

The first variable is the time it takes your customer to decide to buy: it might be a few seconds or half an hour, or it might be tomorrow or next month. Even after you have delivered convincing power points, you may find the customer walks away empty-handed only to come back in an hour and buy the item! In this case, the customer's 'convincer' took an hour to operate.

The second variable is the number of times a customer needs to experience key parts of your power presentation. This means you may have to repeat certain parts several times to match your customer's internal pictures and satisfy their convincer.

Think about your own convincer. Do you walk into the first car showroom you see and buy a car, or do you need several presentations in different showrooms to convince you? Do you buy on impulse or do you need a certain amount of time to think about it? Your convincers may also depend on the type of product and service you are buying. You might take more time to buy a large item like a house than a new pair of shoes.

You will have to use your sales detective techniques to discover the nature of your customers' convincers in each purchasing situation. Keep trying, and always give the customer a business card so that she can get back to you in the future when her convincer kicks in!

Review

Use everything to your advantage to become a top sales producer. You must remember your customers and they must remember you. Starting with a powerful introduction, you can deliver a sales presentation that leads naturally to a satisfied customer.

By delivering power hooks, you can ensure that your customer will remember certain parts more vividly than others: the beginning; the end; any elements that are unusual; anything that's repeated regularly; or things that personally involve the customer. By incorporating these five elements into your sales presentations, you will encourage your customers to remember you and return to you.

Your power hooks have one logical conclusion: a satisfied customer who will buy from you. If your customer does not buy right away, remember the convincer, and give your customer every opportunity to recontact you.

Use all your power hooks – your Sales Mind Matrix, your salesenses, your Sales Focus, your infocentre, Mind Maps, sales detective questions, your sales detective skills, your Sales Compass – use everything to your advantage. Be prepared. You now have an amazing array of new tools: keep them polished by continually using them and you will become a 'super performer'!

Skill Builder 79: power hooks review

On a separate piece of blank paper, summarize this chapter, 'Power Hooks'. You may look back.

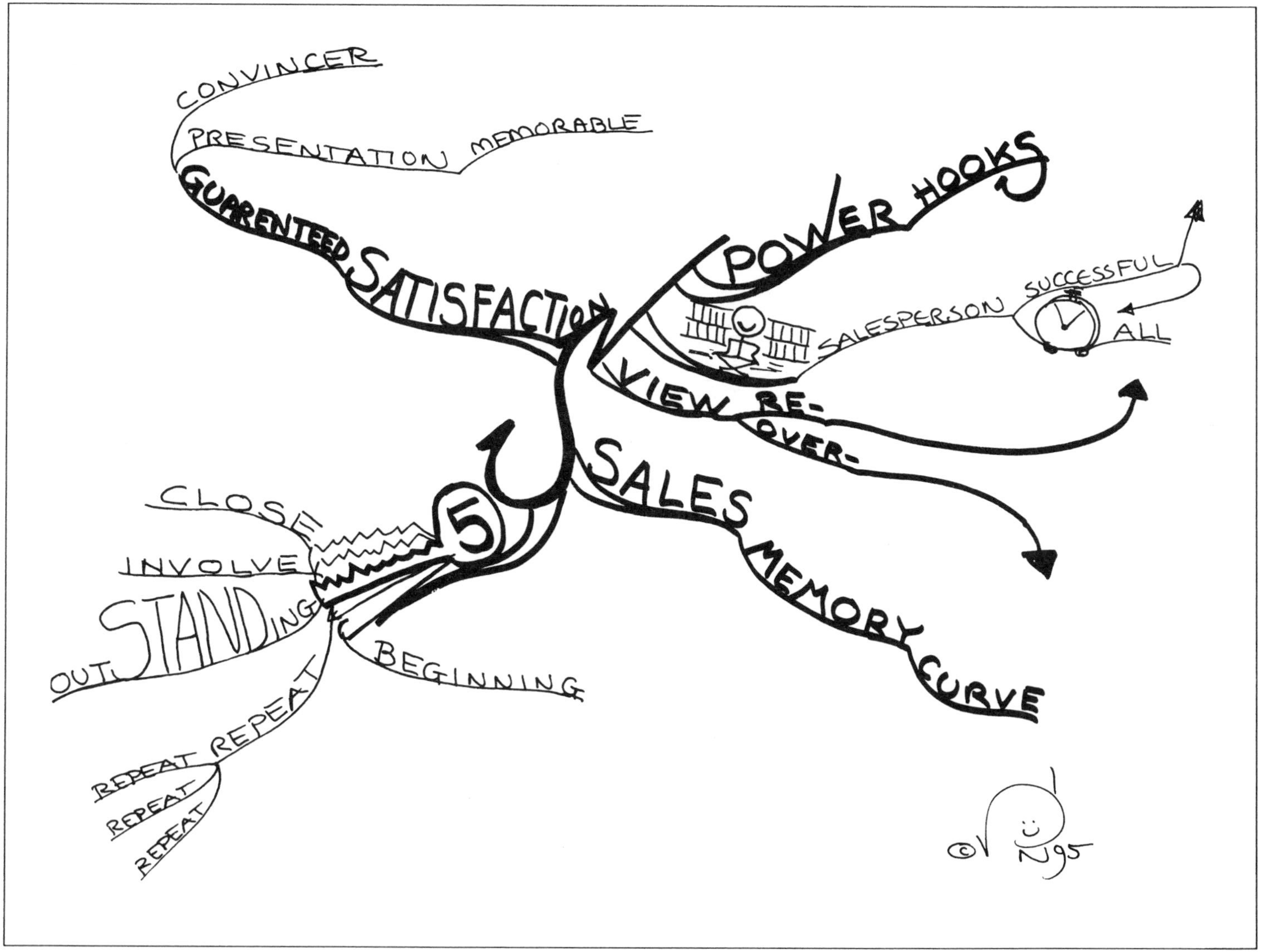

Figure 11.1 Mind Map: power hooks

12 SuperSellf

Discover your SuperSellf, and gain lasting prosperity

A Gemini story

Imagine you had an identical twin – who looks like you, dresses like you, talks like you, behaves like you and even thinks like you. At school you were in the same class, got the same grades and played the same sports. Your twin has the same marital status as you, the same amount of money in the bank and lives in a home like yours.

Your twin does the same work as you, with the same results. You share the same friends, common interests and hobbies. Then, one day you both read *Brain Sell*, and things change!

Your twin read it only once, but you read it again and started practising all the skills outlined in the book. You began to use the *Brain Sell* skills daily. After a few weeks your behaviour and thinking begins to differ from that of your twin for the first time.

Three months pass by and you and your twin swap notes on how well you are both doing at work. Which one of you now has more customers? More sales? The higher income? The more satisfying work? The better chance for promotion? Is you or your twin? Why, it's you! You are excited about the life change and share the following with your twin.

'Remember when we were kids and we went to see our first Superman movie? We saw Clark Kent tear off his shirt and turn into Superman. Remember how excited we were by that idea and how we talked about

221

it for ages? Since I've mastered all the skills in *Brain Sell*, I've become like Superman. Well, not Superman exactly, because I can't fly or do things like that, but I now have new and wonderful powers because of the new way I'm using my brain! My whole life is changing day by day, getting better and better. It's as though I've found my SuperSellf.'

Overview

In this chapter you will meet your amazing SuperSellf and enjoy ultimate prosperity! Your SuperSellf will apply all the skills and knowledge of *Brain Sell* into every aspect of your life. As a result you will become the *best* 'you' – you will become your Supersellf who can communicate better, sell better and live better.

Developing your SuperSellf

You have been selling since the moment you were born. As a hungry baby you cried to gain your mother's attention. You soon learnt to make exactly the right sounds to get food. Yes, we are selling ourselves every day. Many of the things you want require persuading someone else to help you obtain it. We term this part of us our SuperSellf. For many it may be a dormant, for others a very active, 'SuperSellf'. This final chapter is designed to help you get in touch with and develop your SuperSellf.

Let's take a quick test to see how you are doing. Tick off your answers.

Skill Builder 80: how are you doing?

		YES	NO
1.	Are you enjoying every day of your life?		
2.	Do you wake up every morning excited about the day ahead?		
3.	Do you have a life full of activities and friends?		
4.	Are you planning to do something different in the next week?		
5.	Are you living in the house of your dreams?		
6.	Do you have adequate money in the bank?		
7.	Are you eating the right, healthy foods?		
8.	Are you at the ideal weight for your age?		
9.	Do you fell stress-free during your day?		

	YES	NO

10. Are you clearly understood by your customers, peers and family?
11. Are you enjoying good health?
12. Have you planned a future holiday that you are eagerly awaiting?
13. Do you have a wonderful and fulfilling family life?
14. Do you enjoy some sort of physical activity on a weekly basis?
15. Are you interested in the world around you?
16. Are you able to control your intake of alcohol?
17. Do you have favourite places that you enjoy visiting?
18. Are you happy with your physical appearance?
19. Do you live in the present?
20. Do you have dreams that you are looking forward to fulfilling soon?

TOTAL SCORE

If you scored 17 or more 'yeses', you are well on the way to realizing your full potential. If you scored below 17, this chapter will explain how to achieve a perfect score!

Have an outstanding goal

Change is easy and fun to achieve once you understand how your brain works and you start it working for you. Do you have goals in some written form? Goals are important because they start your Sales Mind Matrix working, giving all your mental skills direction and something to work towards. Goals are achieved through aiming your Sales Focus in the right direction.

One of our clients, Max Hung the President of ACER South America, a successful computer company, uses the following three-part formula for motivating himself:

1. Imagine yourself as having reached your goal, and play this mental movie continuously in your mind.
2. Filter out your negative thoughts and focus on your positive ones.
3. Do not rely on external compliments to motivate you; let your own internal thoughts be your motivators.

Does this sound familiar? Motivation is a key to success, and it all starts in your mind! If you have no goals in life, it's difficult to get out of bed in the morning. But, if your goal is to buy a luxury car next year, you will be motivated to go to work each day and save up for the car of your dreams.

Your motivation to achieve your personal goals becomes the framework that guides you every day. Your motivation has nothing to do with what your boss, family or friends want. It's all about the goals *you* set for *yourself*, because only *you* have control over your behaviour.

Sales career goals

Set goals that are realistic yet challenging. Goals need to be specific and measurable. As your sales improve step-by-step, you need to be able to measure your progress. Break your sales career down into short-term, medium and long-term goals.

Skill Builder 81: future goals

Stop for a moment and think about your sales career goals. What do you want to accomplish? Create a Mind Map of your future sales career goals. Put down all your ideas as they come, without concern about whether they are achievable. Simply capture them on the Mind Map. Then, begin to imagine what your life would be like once you had achieved these goals. What will it look like? How will it sound? What will you feel when you achieve your goals?

Now that you have a Mind Map of your goals, go back and colour code them in order of importance. Decide which goals are your short-term goals, those that you would like to complete in the next month. These could be coloured blue. Medium-range goals are for the next six months, and these could be coloured purple. Long-term goals for the next year could be coloured orange. You can colour code each type of goal or use the letters S (short-term), M (medium) and L (long-term).

A typical short-term goal might be to make five follow-up telephone calls per day. A medium-range goal might be to have 100 clients on Mind Map files in six months. A long-term goal might be to have a 100 per cent increase in sales over your current level by a certain date.

Skill Builder 82: getting started

First work with a few goals chosen from your Mind Map, otherwise you won't know where to start or where to place your priorities. Pick three short-term goals for this month, three medium-term goals for the next six months and three long-term goals for the next twelve months. Remember, you will want to start on some small steps towards the long-term goals.

Now list your short-term, medium-term and long-term goals.

Short-term goals (this month)
1. _____
2. _____
3. _____

Medium-term goals (next six months)

1. _____
2. _____
3. _____

Long-term goals (next 12 months)

1. _____
2. _____
3. _____

Some salespeople start worrying about how they might complete their short-term goals and resist getting started. Don't be frustrated. Just take one of your short-term goals and write down at least three steps you can take to achieve this goal. These 'steps' are mini-goals that will help reduce the stress of completing the first short-term goal.

Let's say your short-term goal is to call five clients per day. Step one might be to go through your client Mind Maps and pick five customers to call. Step two would be writing these names and phone numbers in your diary under today's date. Step three would be to call the customers and tick off their names in your diary after you have finished the call. When you have five ticks, you have finished your short-term goal. It's that simple!

Skill Builder 83: short-term goals

In the space below write in your chosen short-term goals and the three steps you intend to take to help you reach each of them.

Short-term goal 1._____

Step 1_____

Step 2_____

Step 3_____

Short-term goal 2._____

Step 1_____

Step 2_____

Step 3_____

Short-term goal 3._____

Step 1_____

Step 2_____

Step 3_____

Belief systems

After determining your goals, the next step towards taking control of your thoughts is to understand your current belief system. These are the thoughts you hold about yourself – the internal pictures on your video screen and soundtracks that you replay continually in your mind. By giving your brain directions, or goals, you will be giving it a new soundtrack to play and new pictures to look for.

To understand your belief system, you must think about what you say to yourself during the day. Do you mentally build yourself up or put yourself down? For instance, when you have spent time with a customer and did not make a sale, does your mental soundtrack go something like this: 'I blew it with that customer, I don't know what's the matter with me' or 'Customers just don't like me. I'm too tall/too short/too fat/too thin/ugly/dumb/forgetful/sloppy/careless'? These are samples of the negative internal soundtracks that many salespeople run daily.

Alternatively, you may give yourself positive feedback: 'How interesting! Now I know why I didn't make that sale' or 'I'm a good learner and each sales presentation makes me better. I'm constantly improving, and using all my skills and knowledge to become the best I can.' Guess which soundtrack works best?

Skill Builder 84: sales tracks

Take a few moments to write down your normal internal soundtrack – both positive and negative – before a sale. Use Figure 12..1.

POSITIVE	NEGATIVE
_____	_____
_____	_____
_____	_____
_____	_____
_____	_____
_____	_____
_____	_____
_____	_____

Figure 12.1 Internal Soundtrack pre-sales presentation

Now turn those soundtracks into pictures. Read the positive sound track and match it with the appropriate mental pictures. Notice how these mental pictures move you towards your goals. Remember that negative pictures will take you away from your goals. Indeed they attract you in the direction you *don't* want to go. You need to have your mental pictures in a 'towards' setting, moving you towards your goals at all times.

Changing mental pictures

Changing to a positive soundtrack is a fast way to change those negative mental pictures. All you have to do is invent positive self-statements. These keep you focused, give you energy and guide you to your goals. Here's how to build a positive self-statement:

1. Always use positive wording. Eliminate negative words like 'no' or 'never'. Rather than tell yourself, 'Don't drop the bottle', keep the statement positive with 'Hold the bottle firmly'.
2. Always use 'I' in your self-statements. Each statement is personal, meant for yourself only. The best approach is to begin each statement with the words 'I am'.
3. Always use the present tense. You want this statement to be something you believe to be true now, not at some future period. For instance, it is far more effective to say to yourself 'I am becoming a successful salesperson' than 'I will become a successful salesperson next year'.

Skill Builder 85: conversion techniques

Now take each negative soundtrack from page 227 and convert it into a positive statement:

Negative thought:_____

Positive statement:

'I am _____

Negative thought:_____

Positive statement:

'I am _____

Negative thought:_____

Positive statement:

'I am _____

Negative thought:_____

Positive statement:

'I am _____

If you have difficulty converting any of these positive thoughts into positive statements, it's a sign that the negative belief needs extra attention. For example, you may write down a positive statement, 'I am making every effort to satisfy all my customers' needs', but shake your head in disbelief. If you have held a negative belief about your selling skills for a long time, the new positive statement will seem unreachable. Be aware of your resistance and ensure that you get the positive statement down on paper.

When you have completed this Skill Builder, go back to each of the negative thoughts on page 227 and draw a red line through it as you erase it from your life. Keep reviewing your positive statements and be aware of your internal sound track. If you hear a new negative thought, convert it immediately into a positive statement.

Affirmations

When you repeat your positive statements, you are affirming your belief in your self, or making an affirmation. Choose one short-, medium- and long-term goal from page 225 for the next Skill Builder on affirmations.

Skill Builder 86: affirmations

In the space below, list a goal and write in a corresponding positive statement or affirmation. For example, if your short-term goal is to make five follow-up calls per day, a positive statement to support the goal would be: 'I am finding time to make my five daily follow-up calls.'

Short-term goal:_____

Positive statement:_____

_____

Medium-term goal:_____

Positive statement:_____

_____

Long-term goal:_____

Positive statement:_____

_____

In Chapter 1, 'Whole-Brain Selling', we introduced the concept of the truth-seeking brain. This applies to 'affirmations' as well. If you have been exposed to 'positive thinking' programmes you will know that they ask you to write affirmations about what you want to be or how you want the world to appear. The problem with this approach is that, often, your affirmations are not true to reality and your truth-seeking brain rejects them. For example, if I were calling on five new customers a day and my affirmation was 'I am getting a wonderful response and orders from customers I call', whereas, in reality, I find this not to be true, my truth-seeking brain would reject this 'positive thinking affirmation' each time I say it!

In *Brain Sell*, we want you to keep your affirmations 'true' so that your truth-seeking brain will accept them and act on them. In the above case I would restate the affirmation in a way that is acceptable: for example, 'Every call teaches me more and draws me closer to success'.

Mental transformers

Make a copy of these goals and positive statements and keep them with your product information Mind Maps, so that you can look at them daily. You should read through your goals at least once in the morning and once in the evening. Each time you read and see your goals, you are taking control of your thinking.

During the workday, you will find it useful to repeat your positive statements; they will act as mental transformers, giving you new energy, focus and clarity of thought.

It is far better to give yourself direction and motivation than to depend on others or to leave your patterns to chance. These positive statements – and the new ones you create over the years – will push you ahead to achieve your life goals.

Goal commercial

Richard developed a process known as Inner Modelling® to help you in the final mind–body link technique. We know that advertising agencies are masters of the art of persuasion. Next time you turn on your television – that coloured, video screen – and see a thirty-second commercial, stop and consider what is happening. A creative, specialized team of individuals, with a large advertising budget, produce this commercial. They send it into your home via your television/video screen and pop in your head, as a new 'inner model'. How effective is this process? Think of your favourite soft drink, beer, fast food or car, then close your eyes and take note of what you experience.

This team of experts are using your Sales Mind Matrix to get their commercial into your mind! Listen to the music on the soundtrack, used to evoke feelings in your multisensory system. If you turn the soundtrack off the commercial will lose much of its power. Through combining multi-sensory information with as many of the Sales Mind Matrix skills as possible they create effective commercials that influence your buying behaviour.

Why not use this technique on yourself? Why not create your own commercial of what you want – your goals? Making a goal commercial combines techniques that we have covered in Parts One, Two, Three and Four – 'Salesenses', 'The Sales Mind Matrix', 'Infoswap', and 'The Sales Compass'.

To put these powerful techniques into practice, preparation is necessary. Consider the following example.

Scripting techniques

With a pen and paper write a script in as much detail as possible on how you will reach your short-term sales goal. Include your actions before reaching the goal, the goal itself and what happens afterwards. Incorporate your positive statements for the end stage. As you think of your script, incorporate what you would see, hear and feel, as you successfully move through all three stages.

For example, one of the short-term goals mentioned earlier was to make five follow-up calls per day, supported by the following positive statements: 'I am making time to make my five daily calls', 'I am learning from each customer I call', and 'I am developing and gaining new insights daily from the experience of calling my five customers'.

The draft script for your goal commercial might read something like this:

I see myself in the office. I notice what I am wearing and I look fabulous. My hair is well groomed. I can smell my favourite cologne that I put on this morning. At home I looked in the mirror, and saw a healthy, happy me. I smiled at myself, which makes me feel even better.

I close my office door so I won't be interrupted. I read the new memo about annual leave and see my name. I know I will be taking my holidays this August and I am excited about my planned trip to Hawaii. As I sit down at the desk, I am aware of the firmness of the chair and hear the buzz of the air conditioner.

I open my diary to today's date. There are the names of the five prospective customers I intend to call about investments with my brokerage firm. I read each name, then take out their Mind Maps from my file. Reviewing Jean Bradsworth's Mind Map, I remember the last time Jean and I spoke; it was about investing in our overseas mutual fund.

I start to dial her number and feel my fingers press the numbers 0202-533593 and, as I hear the phone ring, I put a smile on my face. Jean answers, and I say, 'Jean, this is Donna from Premium Investments. How are you today?' Jean responds, telling me about a party she went to recently. We talk for a few minutes and I tell Jean about the overseas fund and that she can invest small amounts each month. Jean agrees to come in to see me tomorrow. I have completed my first call successfully. I take my pen and write Jean's name in my diary for tomorrow at 10 a.m. I check her name off my call list. I feel good that Jean is coming in. She is keen to start a pension plan and I know I will open an account for her tomorrow.

I read the next name on my list, then make the call. It's another success. Norman Blyth says he will be in on Saturday morning. There is an engaged signal when I call the third name on the list. Both the fourth and fifth calls are successful. Joyce Rosewell asks me to call her again in three weeks. Dan White will see me next Friday to discuss a savings account for his child's education. I try the third call again and this time I leave a message on the answering machine. I have finished my calls and have made three appointments.

I feel pleased with my progress. I think of my goal and how easy it has been to reach it. I mentally review my positive statements: 'I am making time to make my five daily calls', 'I am learning from each customer I call', and 'I am developing and gaining new insights daily from the experience of calling my five customers'.

Then I smile to myself because my positive statements are working for me. I complete my diary and walk back to my manager's office. My manager is pleased with my progress and invites me to have a cup of coffee. I feel great, knowing I am becoming a high producer.

Skill Builder 87: goal commercial

Select a short-term goal, from Skill Builder 86: Affirmations. Study the goal and the positive statements that accompany it. Notice how, in the prepared script above, you used all your senses. You smelled your cologne. You saw yourself in the office, and noticed what you were wearing. You heard the buzz of the air conditioner. You felt really good. This makes the goal commercial seem more realistic and acceptable to your truth-seeking brain, Sales Focus and Sales Mind Matrix. Now write your own script for your own goal commercial in the following space.

Once you have finished the script, read it aloud and make any changes needed to perfect it. Take your final script and read it expressively on to a new cassette tape. This will become your master tape. Label it with the title of the goal and the date your produced it. Then make two copies, one to play in your car if you have a tape deck and one for your home. Keep your master tape stored in a safe place.

Summarized below are the seven steps for preparing your inner modelling tapes:

1. See, hear and feel yourself performing your sales activity.
2. Write down, or dictate into a tape recorder, every detail you can see, hear or feel for your first draft.
3. Break the script into three parts, the action before the sales event, the event and the aftermath.
4. Incorporate as much detail about the event as you can imagine.
5. Picture yourself in control, relaxed and confident as you conduct the sales activity successfully. Include your positive statements in the script.
6. Play back the draft recording, and reread the draft script. Make changes where necessary and complete a final written script.
7. Make a master tape and two copies, so you can listen to your tape frequently.

To use your new goal commercial, find a quiet place where you won't be interrupted. Sit down, close your eyes and take a few deep breaths. Next, go through your relaxation Skill Builder (p. 121) to make sure you are completely relaxed and ready to listen to your goal commercial. Now turn on the tape. Enjoy the goal commercial as though it were really happening. As you listen, you are programming yourself for success and that you will become a high sales producer SuperSellf. Of course, if you listen to your tape in the car, do not do the breathing or relaxation Skill Builder as you may fall asleep. Only do the complete breath and relaxation Skill Builder at home or in a safe place.

Transfer the message!

The first time you hear the goal commercial you will remember a good deal. However, within twenty-four hours you might forget up to 80 per

cent of what you remembered the previous day unless you listen to it
again within 24 hours. The *Brain Sell* secret is to listen to your tape frequently for the first few weeks – every day if possible. This will ensure that
you transfer the message into your long-term memory and that it will be
available whenever you need it. So, listen to your tape as frequently as you
can to achieve the maximum benefit.

When you have finished one tape, go back to your goal Mind Map.
Choose a medium-term goal and Mind Map it. Use it to develop your new
script. Repeat this process for a long-term goal. Soon, you will have three
customized tapes in your library. Keep building your tape library until you
have one tape for each of your goals.

However, you must listen to each tape for at least a week before moving
onto a new one. This gives your mind a chance to absorb and integrate
the messages.

Self-reward

Max Hung from Acer Computers revealed that he rewards himself for
a success by patting himself on the back. When he does something well,
his internal voice says 'Well done Max'. Naturally, Max would like to hear
this from his boss too but, as his boss is in Taiwan, Max relies on his
own internal voice for his positive feedback.

You will need to do the same. When you practise a new skill and
behaviour and do a good job, your internal SuperSellf voice will congratulate you, if you tune in and listen. So give yourself internal reinforcement,
and even small rewards, along the way.

Contacting your SuperSellf

Once you have mastered all the skills in *Brain Sell*, Parts One, Two, Three
and Four and lived them each day, you will have become a SuperSellf. As
a SuperSellf, you live at your full potential, enjoying each moment
of your life and making the most of every opportunity. Your SuperSellf
can set goals and reach them. It has your internal video camera aimed
at the outcomes that will make you a happy human being, living life to
the full.

Skill Builder 88: SuperSellf

On a separate plain sheet of paper, Mind Map what you see as your SuperSellf. Make a vivid central image. Use colours, images, branches and key words (one per branch). Make this a masterpiece. When you have completed it, place it on a wall in your home so that you can see it daily. If you wish to update or redo your SuperSellf Mind Map do so as many times as you like. This SuperSellf Mind Map will help you remind yourself daily of your wonderful, powerful SuperSellf as well as giving your video camera a constant image to aim for.

How does being a SuperSellf help you achieve all the things you want? We have a simple formula: 'You get what you want when the customer gets what she wants.'

Mental score card

What does your customer want? She wants quality information, quality products and services. She also wants a 'quality experience' when dealing with you. Imagine that your customer has a mental score card inside her head with the title 'Quality Experience'. Each time she has a positive or negative experience with you, she checks off the appropriate column on her mental score card. Afterwards she adds up the pluses and minuses. If there are too many negative checks, she probably won't want to see you again!

As a SuperSellf, what type of buying experience do you think your customer will have with you? You can be certain that the ticks will all be in the positive column.

This experience happens with everyone with whom you come into daily contact. Think of all the people you meet – schoolteachers, managers, colleagues, bank clerks, waiters, dry cleaners, waiters, pharmacists – they all have a mental score card at work. How do all these people score you? When they total up their columns, no matter how brief the meeting, will they award high or low marks to their experience with you? Being a SuperSellf ensures that you will always score high marks on their mental score card.

Figure 12.2   Mental score card

Skill Builder 89: contacting your SuperSellf

There will be times when you want to contact your SuperSellf for advice. How best can you do this? The fastest and easiest way is as follows.

Find yourself a space and choose a time when you will not be distracted by interruptions. Take a piece of blank paper and, with your colour markers, develop a Mind Map. The central image will be the question you want your SuperSellf to answer. Make sure that the question is in image or picture form. Don't force the answers but wait until the ideas and solutions flow on to the paper. Obviously, your hand will be writing and drawing these ideas and solutions, but you will be guided by your inner voice, or inner self – your Super-Sellf. There is a subtle difference here between your normal conscious self and your SuperSellf. Time, patience and practice will help you to distinguish between the two.

Sometimes your SuperSellf gives an instant answer. There will be times when you will have to wait while your SuperSellf works on the best response. In such cases keep your Mind Map readily available, on your desk or next to your bed. The answers will come, maybe in a day or so, and you will want to record them instantly.

How did you do? If you have not got all the answers, wait and return in a few hours or tomorrow. Keep all your SuperSellf Mind Maps in a separate Mind Map folder for future reference.

Set aside some quiet, uninterrupted time each week for reviewing your SuperSellf Mind Maps. You will be delighted as you 'update' your progress and gain new insights into the exciting adventure with your SuperSellf.

Skill Builder 90: advanced methods

Once you have used the Mind Mapping technique to contact your SuperSellf for a few months, you will be ready for the advanced method. Here you contact your SuperSellf on your internal video screen. Hold the central image of your question on your screen, and watch the answers develop on the branches.

Alternatively, if you prefer to hold an inner dialogue with your SuperSellf, you can ask it a series of pertinent questions, such as:

● 'SuperSellf, what is a quick way to ...?'
● 'SuperSellf, what is the next step in ...?'
● 'SuperSellf, how can I better ...?'
● 'SuperSellf, how best can I approach ...?'

Your SuperSellf will answer in different ways, maybe with images or with an inner dialogue or simply a hunch. As you learn to tune into your SuperSellf you will recognize the responses.

Passwords to success

Soon you will know the answers to the above questions without even asking them. It's similar to driving a car, being on automatic pilot. You know exactly what to do from turning on the engine to driving to your destination. Your SuperSellf will soon be your automatic pilot through enriched, happy and creative living.

Our final words on *Brain Sell* sales techniques are probably the most important. All the advice you have gained from reading *Brain Sell* and from contacting your SuperSellf will require you to *take action*. The secret to all results is in the implementation. *'Keep TAKING ACTION'* must be your constant passwords to success.

This is not the end; it is the beginning of an exciting journey. Continue to learn and practise your new *Brain Sell* skills. This way, you will grow and develop into your magnificent SuperSellf.

Review

In this final section of *Brain Sell*, you discovered your amazing SuperSellf, a sub-personality waiting to manifest itself in your daily life.

The focus of this section was on the importance of knowing where you are headed and having the corresponding goals to get you there. Once you set your goals you went through a detailed process, taking your short-, medium- and long-term goals from the Mind Mapping stage, through drafting, incorporating them into your thought process, influencing your belief systems and finally ending up as a goal commercial.

The advertising industry uses commercials to motivate consumers into buying an endless array of goods and services. Now you are armed with your customized goal commercial, whenever you need to be self-motivated, all you have to do is simply play it! This develops your ability to rely more on your self and less on external motivators to move you ahead.

Finally you discovered the secret that all salespeople need to understand if they are to be successful: 'You get what you want when the customer gets what he wants.' By scoring high marks on your customers' internal mental score card, you will ensure that this formula works for you.

As you develop these and all the other techniques covered in *Brain Sell*, your selling skills and sales will increase. You will live and enjoy your newly found status, that of a true SUPERSELLF.

Skill Builder 91: SuperSellf review

On a separate piece of blank paper, Mind Map this chapter, 'SuperSellf'. Do not look back!

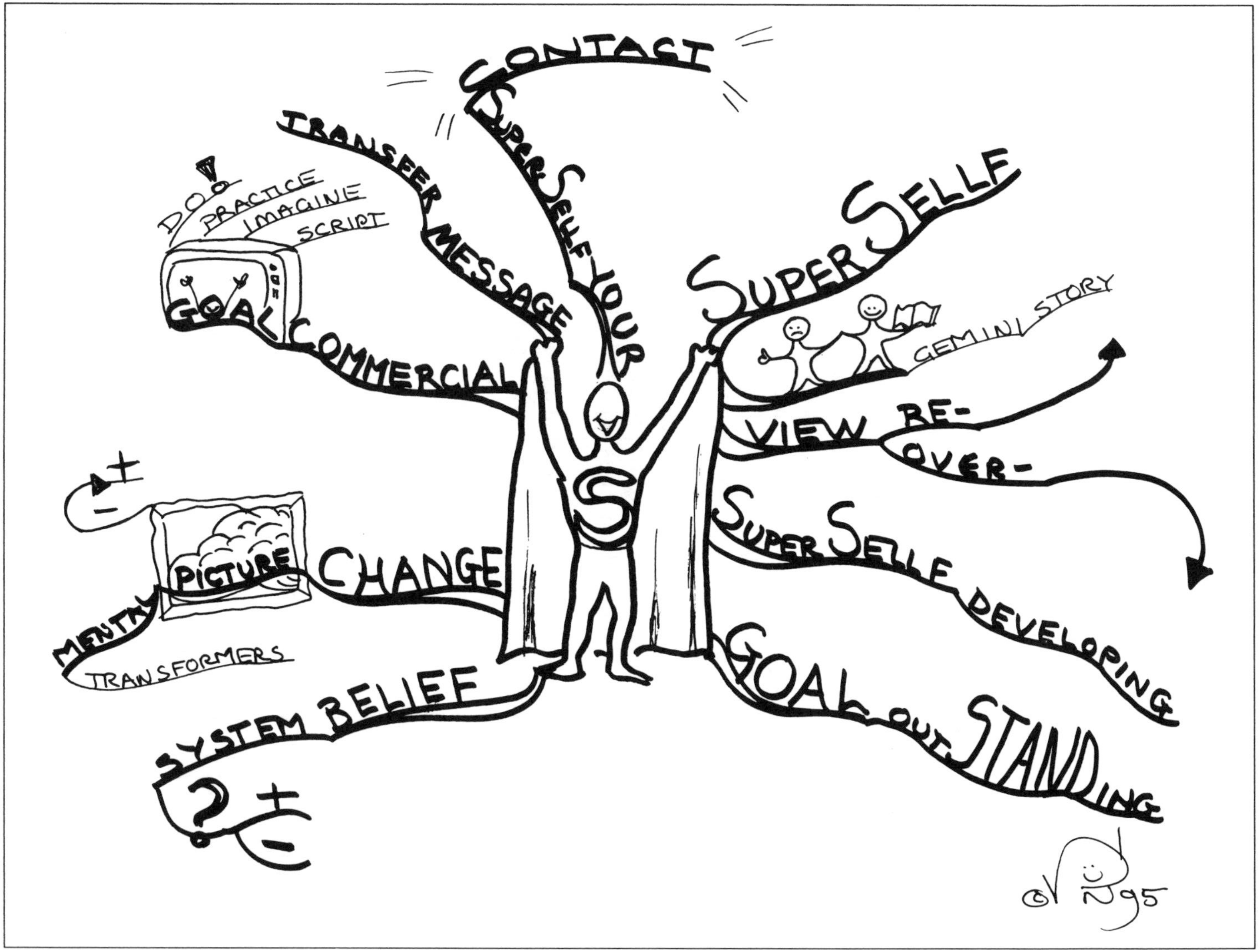

Figure 12.3 Mind Map: SuperSellf

APPENDICES

Appendix A:

Sales management

To help you manage your sales, we have included a short section on personal sales management, with three Skill Builders.

Skill Builder 92: sales behaviour grid

Below is a grid of the new skills and behaviours found in Parts One, Two, Three and Four, each with its corresponding page reference.

Each new skill and behaviour needs to be practised. The more you practise the sooner you will become a SuperSellf.

To keep a record of the times you practise each new skill and behaviour, tick off each practice under the heading 'practised'. With each skill you practise, you will receive 'reinforcement'! This could be from your sales manager or a satisfied customer, or just an internal good feeling. Each time you experience reinforcement, tick it off against the respective skill/behaviour, in the 'reinforced' column.

The final column is headed 'mastered'. When you have mastered the new skill or behaviour tick off the appropriate column and move on to the next skill or behaviour. This will give you a visual record of your progress as you master each new skill.

SKILL/BEHAVIOUR	PART	PAGE	PRACTISED	REINFORCED	MASTERED
1. State of excellence	One	31			
2. Sales Matrix	One	14			
3. Salesenses	One	32			
4. Truth-seeking brain	One	22			
5. Names and faces	One	46			
6. Stance	Two	111			
7. Voice	Two	117			
8. Infoswap	Two	78			
9. Mind Mapping	Two	90			
10. Physical health	Two	122			
11. Relaxation	Two	121			
12. Detective questions	Three	148			
13. Sales compass	Three	169			
14. Complete picture	Three	161			
15. Match brain pictures	Three	164			
16. Aim frame	Four	196			
17. Observation skills	Four	201			
18. Five power hooks	Four	211			
19. Metal check	Four	197			
20. Every sale twice	Four	196			

Skill Builder 93: tracking sales performance

The following three pages of graph paper are for your sales graphs. Make a horizontal axis for time (days, weeks or months) and a vertical axis for sales measured in either sales volumes or sales commissions.

Skill Builder 94: sales compasses

Following the graph pages are a series of blank Sales Compasses (see page 169 for explanation). Use the blanks to analyse your own sales, or those of other high sales achievers, with whom you might be working.

These completed Sales Compasses will prove invaluable to your improved sales performance. Feedback is crucial to success. Your sales performance will not improve if you repeat the same sales behaviours incorrectly! But studying your completed Sales Compasses, and deciding how to improve, will make all the difference!

	CUSTOMER COVERED: YES NO	SALESPERSON MATCHED: YES NO	SALESPERSON ADDED: YES NO
SENSORY DATA			
Sound			
Sight			
Smell			
Taste			
Touch			
MENTAL SKILLS			
Numbers			
Words			
Logic			
Lists			
Details			
Pictures			
Imagination			
Colour			
Rhythm			
Space			

	CUSTOMER COVERED: YES NO	SALESPERSON MATCHED: YES NO	SALESPERSON ADDED: YES NO
SENSORY DATA			
Sound			
Sight			
Smell			
Taste			
Touch			
MENTAL SKILLS			
Numbers			
Words			
Logic			
Lists			
Details			
Pictures			
Imagination			
Colour			
Rhythm			
Space			

Brain Sell **Compasses**

	CUSTOMER COVERED: YES NO	SALESPERSON MATCHED: YES NO	SALESPERSON ADDED: YES NO
SENSORY DATA			
Sound			
Sight			
Smell			
Taste			
Touch			
MENTAL SKILLS			
Numbers			
Words			
Logic			
Lists			
Details			
Pictures			
Imagination			
Colour			
Rhythm			
Space			

	CUSTOMER COVERED: YES NO	SALESPERSON MATCHED: YES NO	SALESPERSON ADDED: YES NO
SENSORY DATA			
Sound			
Sight			
Smell			
Taste			
Touch			
MENTAL SKILLS			
Numbers			
Words			
Logic			
Lists			
Details			
Pictures			
Imagination			
Colour			
Rhythm			
Space			

Brain Sell **Compasses**

	CUSTOMER COVERED: YES NO	SALESPERSON MATCHED: YES NO	SALESPERSON ADDED: YES NO
SENSORY DATA			
Sound			
Sight			
Smell			
Taste			
Touch			
MENTAL SKILLS			
Numbers			
Words			
Logic			
Lists			
Details			
Pictures			
Imagination			
Colour			
Rhythm			
Space			

	CUSTOMER COVERED: YES NO	SALESPERSON MATCHED: YES NO	SALESPERSON ADDED: YES NO
SENSORY DATA			
Sound			
Sight			
Smell			
Taste			
Touch			
MENTAL SKILLS			
Numbers			
Words			
Logic			
Lists			
Details			
Pictures			
Imagination			
Colour			
Rhythm			
Space			

Brain Sell Compasses

Appendix B:

The Brain Sellers' Network

The Brain Sellers' Network gives an opportunity to learn and earn more using *Brain Sell* technologies and products.

To contact Tony Buzan or Richard Israel or to get more information on the worldwide opportunities afforded by the Brain Sellers' Network, write to:

Brain Sellers' Network
PO Box 630503
Miami
Florida 33163
USA
Fax: 1(305) 931 7688

For information on *Brain Sell* courses contact the Buzan Centre addresses below:

Europe

The Buzan Centre Ltd
37 Waterloo Road
Bournemouth
Dorset BH9 1BD
UK
Tel: (01202) 533593
Fax: (01202) 534572

North America

The Buzan Centres USA Inc.
415 Federal Highway
Lake Park
Florida 33403
USA
Tel: 1(407) 881 0188 or (800) Y-MIND MAP
Fax: 1(407) 845 3210

Also by Tony Buzan

Books

The Mind Map Book: Radiant Thinking   The comprehensive guide to Mind Mapping® by its originator. Exciting new ways to use and improve your memory, concentration and creativity in planning and structuring thought on all levels.

Use Your Head   The classic BBC best seller, which has sold over a million copies. Foundation learning skills and Mind Mapping explained by their inventor. Latest information on your brain's functioning, enabling you to Learn How to Learn more effectively.

Use Your Memory   An encyclopaedia of brain-related memory techniques. Provides easy-to-manage techniques for remembering names, faces, places, jokes, telephone numbers and everything you want or need to remember.

Speed/Range Reading   Establish a range of reading speeds up to 10 000 wpm with good comprehension. Self-checks and practical exercises throughout.

Make the Most of Your Mind (paperback); *Harnessing the Parabrain* (hardback)   A complete course-in-a-book dealing with reading, memory, number skills, logic, vision, listening and study. Builds to the complete Mind Map Organic Study Technique.

Master Your Memory   Expands your memory systems from 10 to 10 000! Also provides basic data in 12 subject areas, including art, literature, science and languages.

Memory Vision   A 'work book' to go with *Master Your Memory*, in which to record your 10 000 knowledge databases.

Spore One (poetry)   Reality seen through many facets. A poetic 'work-out' for your brain.

Books with other authors

Get Ahead by Vanda North with Tony Buzan. A practical, easy and inviting introduction to Mind Mapping. How to apply it to your life to 'Get Ahead' quicker; also includes a 2-week 'Just Do It' new habit section.

Lessons From the Art of Juggling by Michael J. Gelb and Tony Buzan. Juggling is a delightful metaphor for living and learning. You will discover the secrets of transforming failure into success and mastering the art of relaxed concentration. Learn to juggle and how to learn.

Brain Power for Kids by Lana Israel with Tony Buzan. Lana, the 1994 Brain

Trust Brain of the Year, explains how to make schoolwork easier by applying the Mind Map to reports, essays, research, note-taking and exams.

Audio tapes

Each 45-minute cassette is accompanied by a booklet. The seven tapes are: *Buzan on the Brain; Buzan on Memory; Buzan on Radiant Thinking and Creativity; Buzan on Mind Mapping; Buzan on Reading; Buzan on Success;* and *Buzan on Body and Mind.*

In this brand new 'Buzan on' audio series, Tony is interviewed by Vanda North on a range of topics. Each audio is fast-paced Buzan wisdom, ending with ten Action Points for improvement in each specific area.

Video tapes

If At First... (one 25-minute tape with trainer booklet) Many organizations and individuals say they encourage risk-taking and making mistakes. But it is not so simple to cast aside an anxiety which has been carried with us since schooldays. In '*If At First...*', Buzan helps us look at the fear of failure as an event on our learning curve. Charthouse's film gives rise to group discussions that shift people's attitudes and guarantees that they become more creative and successful.

Mindpower (two 25-minute videos with a work book) Mind Mapping applications for today's business. In the BBC's new technologically superb video-led course Tony Buzan teaches you how to use Mind Maps to clarify your thinking and make better use of your mental resources.

Developing Family Genius (four 70-minute videos) A complete, entertaining and highly participative course for the entire family or individuals, where Tony Buzan introduces you to the wonders of the human brain. Learn how to: learn; think; remember; read fast with comprehension; study effectively and easily take and pass exams.

Get Ahead (a 60-minute video with a booklet) In this fun-to-watch video, Tony introduces Lana Israel, a 16-year-old student. Lana takes students on a step-by-step demonstration of how to apply Mind Mapping to improve study, revise for exams and enhance memory.

The Enchanted Loom (a 60-minute video) Classic documentary on the brain, featuring interviews with the world's major contributors to the field. Devised by Buzan and including his pioneer work with learning-disadvantaged children.

Other products

Mind Maps® plus Software Programme   The new computer thinking tool may be used on any PC compatible with VGA running DOS. The first Mind Map computer program doubles creativity and allows flexible and instantaneous manifestation of ideas and logs levels of thought. Can translate to linear for the non-Mind Map literate.

Mind Map Pads/Kits   Each printing of a Mind Map pad is covered with a limited edition Mind Map. The kit contains an A3 and A4 pad, a Buzan 4-colour pen and highlighters.

Body and Soul Poster (85 x 67 cm)   A limited edition, master Mind Map style poster depicting, in a surrealist manner, all the principles of Radiant Thinking. Each numbered copy is signed by the Swedish artist, Ulf Ekberg.

SEM³   This user-friendly laminated chart of the Self-enhancing Master Memory Matrix enables the *Master Your Memory* reader to memorize up to 10 000 items with ease.

The Universal Personal Organizer (UPO)   This unique approach to self/time-management is a diary system, based on the techniques created and taught by Tony Buzan and the Buzan Centres. The UPO is a living system that grows with you and gives a comprehensive picture of your life, your desires, and your business and family functions.

The Mind Map Map   This introduction to Mind Maps offers a 'How To' and 'Question and Answer' on one side and a multi-coloured Mind Map on Mind Mapping on the other.

Training courses in Mental Literacy and Radiant Thinking

Full range of Radiant Thinking skills for study, work and life include courses prepared for: individuals from five years of age upwards; families; clubs, organizations and committees; people of all intellectual levels and abilities including the learning-disabled; corporations of any size, including directors, managers and all staff.

There are five Radiant Thinking Training Programmes.

Radiant Thinking   This foundation course allows you to tap the full creative potential of your brain. Application of the thought organization technique called a Mind Map® to a range of life and business needs, i.e. problem solving; studying; communication and planning, including creative thinking and memory.

Radiant Remembering   Practical application of the memory principles, rhythms and systems for remembering data, lists, faces and anything else! Saves time, money and embarrassment.

Radiant Reading   Climb over that stack of information! Make informed decisions by applying research about the eyes and brain to manage all kinds of reading material with speed, efficiency, comprehension and appreciation.

Radiant Speaking   Three leaders in the field give step-by-step practical applications for effective speaking with confidence and enjoyment under any circumstances.

Radiant Success   Remove fear from failure when you know the TEFCAS brain compatible process. Learn how you learn.

Radiant Thinking training programme formats

Open Introductory Radiant Thinking Programmes   Usually conducted over a weekend, and introducing Mind Mapping, Radiant Thinking, Reading and Memory Skills. All ages welcome.

Open Radiant Thinking Programmes   One day, including a course book, focusing on either Radiant Thinking (Mind Maps), Remembering, Reading, Speaking or Success.

Company Radiant Thinking   Radiant Thinking courses are specially customized to be immediately applicable for groups of ten plus people in any one, or more, of the Radiant Thinking Programmes. The five courses can stand alone, or be combined with each other or existing company courses.

Radiant Thinking Instructor Programmes   In-depth training, licensing you to teach the Radiant Thinking Programmes. Pre-course preparation prior to a full week of training. Competency based. Certification through to full diploma.

For information on *Brain Sell* and other training courses, products to learn how to learn and the current information pack, contact the Buzan Centre addresses on p. 251, enclosing a large (10 x 30 cm/8 x 12 in) stamped self-addressed envelope.

The Mind Mappers' Society

You are invited to join this society, founded by Tony Buzan and organized by Buzan Centres Limited. The society's specific objective is to raise money for research into thinking and learning through The Brain Trust, charity number 1001012. Life membership to the Mind Mappers' Society is by introduction (this is yours!) and upon payment of at least £5.00/$10.00. For this you will receive a membership card, a lapel pin, knowledge that you have assisted research into thinking and learning, and fellowship into the global body of Mind Mappers. To join, send your donation to Buzan Centres Limited, along with your full name and address.

Further Reading

Alies, Roger, *You are the Message*. Doubleday, New York, 1989.

Albreacht, Karl and Zemke, Ron, *Service America!* Dow Jones Irwin, Homewood, 1985.

Anderson, J. R., *Cognitive Psychology and its Implications*. W. H. Freeman Co., New York, 1985.

Ashcraft, M. H., *Human Memory and Cognition*. Foresman & Co., Glenview, 1989.

Borysenko, Joan, *Minding the Body, Mending the Mind*. Addison Wesley, Reading, 1987.

Bandler, Richard, *Using Your Brain – for a CHANGE*. Real People Press, Moab, 1985.

Buzan, Tony, and Keene, Raymond, *Buzan's Book of Genius*. Stanley Paul, London, 1994.

Buzan, Tony, *The Mind Map Book*. B.B.C. Books, London, 1993.

Buzan, Tony, *Use Your Memory*. B.B.C. Books, London, 1995.

Daehler, M. W. and Bukatko, D., *Cognitive Development*. Alfred A. Knopf,· New York, 1985.

Diamond, Stuart, *The Double Brain*. Churchill Livingstone, London, 1972.

Friedland, Dion, Israel, Richard and Lynch, Edith, *People Productivity in Retail*. Lehabar Friedman Books, New York, 1980.

Gazzaniga, Michael S., *Mind Matters*. Houghton Mifflin Co., Boston, 1988.

Gendlin, Eugene T., *Focusing*. Everest House, New York, 1978.

Hooper, J. and Teresi, D., *The Three-pound Universe*. Dell Publishing Co., New York, 1986.

Israel, Richard, Huckabee, Bill and Berry, Peter, 'How To Think', *People & Profits*, July 1981, Johannesburg.

Israel, Richard and Crane, Julianne, *Peak Sales Vision*. Winterstreet Inc., Miami, 1995.

Israel, Richard, North, Vanda with Buzan, Tony, *Radiant Speaking*. Buzan Centres Ltd., Bournemouth, 1993.

Luria, A., *The Mind of a Mnemonist*. Harvard University Press, Cambridge, 1968.

Matlin, M. W., *Cognition*. Holt, Reinhart, & Winston, New York, 1989.

Mintzberg, Henry, 'Planning on the left side and managing on the right'. *Harvard Business Review*, Boston, July–August 1976.

North, Vanda with Buzan, Tony, *Get Ahead*. BC Books, Bournemouth, 1991.

Rackham, Neil, *SPIN Selling*. McGraw-Hill Inc., New York, 1988.

Restak, Richard MD, *The Brain*. Bantam Books, New York, 1984.

Russell, Peter, *The Brain Book*. Plume, New York, 1979.

Sperry, Roger W., 'Hemispheric Deconnection and Unity in Conscious Awareness', *Scientific American* 23, 723–33.

Springer, S. P., and Deutsch, G., *Left Brain, Right Brain* revised edition. W. H. Freeman & Co., New York, 1985.

Sternberg, Robert J., *The Triarchic Mind*, Viking, New York, 1988.

Tack, Alfred, *Increase Your Sales the Tack Way*. Gower, Aldershot, 1990.

Tart, T. C., *Altered states of consciousness*. John Wiley & Sons, New York, 1969.

Toffler, Alvin, *Powershift*. Bantam, New York, 1991.

Waston, David L. and Tharp, Roland G., *Self-Directed Behavior*. Brooks/Cole Belmont, 1985.

Index